Dementia Research and Care

CAN BIG DATA HELP?

Edited by
Geoff Anderson and Jillian Oderkirk

Please cite this publication as:
Anderson, G. and J. Oderkirk (eds.) (2015), *Dementia Research and Care: Can Big Data Help?*, OECD Publishing, Paris.
http://dx.doi.org/10.1787/9789264228429-en

ISBN 978-92-64-22841-2 (print)
ISBN 978-92-64-22842-9 (PDF)

The statistical data for Israel are supplied by and under the responsibility of the relevant Israeli authorities. The use of such data by the OECD is without prejudice to the status of the Golan Heights, East Jerusalem and Israeli settlements in the West Bank under the terms of international law.

Corrigenda to OECD publications may be found on line at: *www.oecd.org/about/publishing/corrigenda.htm*.

Foreword

G8 countries made a bold and ambitious commitment to find a cure or disease-modifying therapy for dementia by 2025. This commitment has been a catalyst for global action to improve the health and social care of people with dementia and to accelerate innovation to discover new therapies to prevent or limit this disease. International collaboration is critical to encourage multi-disciplinary, cross-border research and to enhance knowledge transfer of effective solutions. The UK Department of Health along with G7 countries, the OECD and the WHO are leading a series of projects, workshops and events in 2014-15 toward solutions to different aspects of this challenge, ranging from drug discovery through to better health care.

New opportunities are already in sight. Current progress in the development of electronic health care data enables a quantum leap forward in our understanding of dementia patients and their care. When these "broad data" can be combined with "deep data" including genetic markers, lifestyles and environments, we will hold the key to unlocking the strategies to prevent dementia, to slow its progress, and to promote patients' quality of life and high-quality caring services that meet patients' needs. This is what leading researchers and academics, industry and non-government experts and policy makers from OECD countries agreed at a workshop hosted by the OECD, the Ontario Brain Institute (OBI) and the Institute of Health Policy, Management and Evaluation (IHPME) on 14-15 September 2014, in Toronto (Canada).

Current progress is encouraging but there is no room for complacency. Opportunities should be pursued further, for example through efforts to develop a centre of global excellence to tackle outstanding technical, legal and data challenges and to support countries in enabling the use of data needed to find a cure and improve care. Crucially, better metrics to compare countries' performance over time should be developed, and opportunities to develop pilot studies that demonstrate the power of linking "broad and deep" data should be encouraged.

This publication brings together an impressive set of papers on the development and use of data, contributed by experts from industry, academia and government. Our hope is that they will offer new insight into the opportunities and challenges in making "broad and deep" data a reality – from funding to data standards, to data sharing, to new analytics, to protecting privacy, and to engaging with stakeholders and the public. We look forward to a future when we can look back at this workshop and be proud of its contribution to ensuring that big data are effectively used for cure discovery, as well as to support and evaluate policies to better care for individuals with dementia.

ACKNOWLEDGMENTS

This workshop was jointly organised by the Ontario Brain Institute (OBI), the Institute of Health Policy, Management and Evaluation (IHPME) and the OECD. The efforts of Geoffrey Anderson (IHPME), Adalsteinn Brown (IHPME), Francesca Colombo (OECD), Richard Johnson (BIAC), Kirk Nylen (OBI), Jillian Oderkirk (OECD), Jenine Paul (OBI), Elettra Ronchi (OECD), Donald Stuss (OBI), Isabelle Vallard (OECD), and Jeremy Veillard (IHPME) are gratefully acknowledged.

The OECD, OBI and IHME would like to thank all of the workshop participants for their contributions to a productive discussion and, in particular, to thank the experts who authored the papers that are included in this publication and who prepared presentations and participated in panels to inform the debate. Geoffrey Anderson (IHPME) and Jillian Oderkirk (OECD) were the editors of this manuscript and their contributions are appreciated.

Table of contents

Tables

Figures

Acronyms and abbreviations

ACOVE	Assessing Care of Vulnerable Elders
AD	Alzheimer's disease
ADGC	Alzheimer's Disease Genetics Consortium
ADNI	Alzheimer's Disease Neuroimaging Initiative
AMA	American Medical Association
BHAG	Big Hairy Audacious Goal
CEOi	CEO Initiative on Alzheimer's Disease
CIHI	Canadian Institute for Health Information
CSF	Cerebrospinal fluid
CT	Computed tomography
CV	Cardiovascular
DLB	Dementia with Lewy bodies
DNA	Deoxyribonucleic acid
DWG	Dementia Measures Work Group
EBI	European bioinformatics Institute
EHR	Electronic health record
FTD	Fronto-temporal dementia
GAP	Global Alzheimer's Platform
IHI	Institute for Healthcare Improvement
IHPME	Institute of Health Policy, Management and Evaluation
iPS	Induced pluripotent stem
JPND	Joint Programme Neurodegenerative Disease Research
MRI	Magnetic resonance imaging
MS	Multiple sclerosis
NHS	National Health System
NICE	National Institute for Health and Care Excellence
NIH	National Institutes of Health
OBI	Ontario Brain Institute

PROM	Patient reported outcome measure
R&D	Research and development
RNA	Nuclear ribonucleic acid
SNP	Single nucleotide polymorphism
US FDA	United States Food and Drug Administration
WES	Whole-exome sequence
WHO	World Health Organization

Executive summary

The burden of dementia on individuals, families, communities and health care systems is rising globally as world populations age. The demand for a therapy to prevent dementia or to slow its progress is great, but traditional approaches to therapeutic discovery have not been successful. New approaches are needed to discover a cure or disease-modifying therapy and to improve health and social care services for the growing number of people with dementia.

The Organisation for Economic Co-operation and Development (OECD), the Ontario Brain Institute (OBI) and the Institute of Health Policy, Management and Evaluation (IHPME) of the University of Toronto jointly hosted a workshop on 14-15 September 2014 to advance international discussion of the opportunities and challenges, as well as successful strategies, of sharing and linking the massive amounts of population-based health and health care data that are routinely collected (broad data) with detailed clinical and biological data (deep data) to create an international resource for research, planning, policy-development, and performance improvement.

Dementia is a complex condition resulting from a set of diseases, each with a complex interplay between genes and the environment. Linking broad and deep data creates a more complete history of patients' characteristics, treatments and outcomes. Such data enable discovering which treatments work best for particular patient groups, which are unsafe or harmful, the resources required to deliver the treatments and the contexts within which results are optimal.

Moving forward will require active involvement of the research community, the private sector and the public. Researchers and research institutions will need to explore ways to better share ideas and to create partnerships. Creating a culture of open science will require understanding and addressing the concerns of scientists and partnering with the institutions that employ and support researchers. There is also an important role for businesses and the private sector. This will include the pharmaceutical industry but also broader private sector interests in health and social care. In the context of big data, private sector involvement should also include the large number of companies and businesses that are involved in the production and analysis of large data. Finally, but perhaps most importantly, is the involvement of the public in strategies to enable data to support research and care. Dementia is a condition that does not just affect patients but also their families and caregivers and ultimately, given its scope, economies and the social fabric. Engaging the public in understanding the potential value of linking data and the balance between that and legitimate and fundamental concerns about privacy is essential to moving forward.

The workshop presentations and discussions identified several factors that would support efforts to enable broad and deep data to contribute to dementia cure and care:

- Creating a culture of open science and addressing issues that limit data sharing between scientists and research groups.

- Developing data standards to improve quality and meta data about the strengths and weaknesses of different data sources to support data linkages.
- Developing new approaches to analytics.
- Incentivising partnerships between the public and private sectors.
- Incorporating strong data governance that protects patients' privacy.
- Involving patients and the public in a discussion about the benefits and risks of data use and the safeguards in place to mitigate those risks.
- Developing comparable health system performance indicators and projections of the costs of dementia care to build support for investments in data and research.
- Undertaking case studies of linking broad and deep data to provide evidence of the benefits for dementia treatment and care.

A comprehensive strategy that creates an infrastructure that supports efforts to link broad and deep data in all interested countries is needed. The strategy should encourage specific collaborative efforts that can better define the value of broad and deep data linkages. This work will build upon and support existing efforts around discovery research in dementia and will help to ensure that there are international and national efforts focused on performance measurement and supporting improvement in systems of health and social care for all those affected by dementia.

Key next steps that emerged from the meeting included:

- Pursue the possibility to develop an international centre of excellence or a clearing house to discuss issues around good practice in data governance, privacy protection and data standards to support national development of broad and deep data and to support multi-country projects involving data sharing.
- Develop international benchmarks and comparisons of the performance of health systems in caring for dementia patients, starting with the identification of key performance measures, and then investigating and comparing data sources, developing internationally comparable definitions and piloting indicator development.
- Pursue an international project involving the linkage of broad and deep data as a pilot or proof of concept study to demonstrate the benefits of this type of data to dementia research and care and as a test bed to work through challenges and develop solutions for future projects.

Chapter 1

Broad and deep data for dementia: Opportunities for care and cure, challenges and next steps

Geoffrey Anderson, Adalsteinn Brown, Francesca Colombo, Jillian Oderkirk, Elettra Ronchi, Donald T. Stuss and Jeremy Veillard[1]

The burden of dementia on individuals, families, communities and health care systems is rising globally as world populations age. The Toronto workshop on 14-15 September 2014 identified opportunities and challenges, as well as successful strategies, of sharing and linking the massive amounts of population-based health and health care data that are routinely collected (broad data) with detailed clinical and biological data (deep data) to create an international resource for research, planning, policy-development, and performance improvement. While the potential benefits to dementia cure and care are great, there are significant challenges related to data quality, data sharing and access to data; the protection of privacy; public engagement; and funding and incentives. Moving forward will require active involvement of governments, the research community, the private sector and the public. Next steps could include pursuing the possibility of creating a global centre of excellence to share and promote best practices; developing metrics to compare countries' performance over time, and conducting pilot studies to demonstrate the value of linking "broad and deep" data to discovering better therapies and improving health care services.

Countries across the world are facing the challenge of developing and implementing comprehensive strategies for understanding dementia in terms of its etiology and epidemiology, its impact on the affected individuals and their families and on health and social care systems.

Reflecting the current global commitment, a call for immediate strategies and innovations to improve the quality of life of those affected by dementia and for efforts to develop disease-modifying therapies or a cure by 2025 were articulated in the December 2013 G8 communiqué (G8, 2013).

The September 2014 workshop in Toronto was jointly organised and sponsored by the OECD, the Ontario Brain Institute (OBI) and the Institute for Health Policy, Management and Evaluation (IHPME) of the University of Toronto. The aim of the workshop was to advance international discussion of the opportunities and challenges, as well as successful strategies, of sharing and linking the massive amounts of population-based health and health care data that are routinely collected (broad data) with detailed clinical and biological data (deep data) to create an international resource for research, planning, policy-development, and performance improvement.

A recent OECD paper has pointed out that big data are at the heart of the knowledge-based economy and are an important engine for innovation and growth across many sectors (OECD, 2015) and an international workshop identified the development and use of big data as key factors in advancing dementia research (OECD, 2014). The value of big data in dementia, and in particular of broad and deep data, is driven by the benefits of a multi-disciplinary approach to modern health research; the complex, multifactorial nature of dementia; and the impact dementia has on both health and social policy.

Modern health research can be seen as having four disciplinary pillars – basic science, clinical studies, health services/policy research and public or population health research. Although perhaps a simplification, it can be argued that the first two pillars primarily use and produce deep data (detailed biological and clinical data on a relatively small number of research subjects) and the second two pillars use and produce broad data (limited amounts of outcome and exposure data on large populations). Linking broad and deep data will create a resource that allows scientists from different disciplines to collaborate, apply innovative methods and develop new insights. Linking data requires information to locate the same individuals or groups of individuals within multiple broad and deep datasets, so that the data can be accurately merged to create a more complete history of patients' characteristics, treatments and outcomes. Such data enable discovering which treatments work best for particular patient groups, which are unsafe or harmful, the resources required to deliver the treatments and the contexts within which results are optimal.

Dementia is complex to study because it is not one disease – it is certainly not just Alzheimer's. Despite that inherent challenge, there are two common features of the neurodegenerative diseases that lead to dementia. One is that the vast majority of cases of dementia are caused by a complex interplay between genomic, epigenomic, and environmental causes. Another is that individuals with dementia have varying trajectories of progression from pre-clinical to progressive cognitive decline to terminal status. The gene-environment causal pathway and the importance of characterising long-term disease progression and outcomes argue for linking broad and deep data to support research for a cure.

Dementia is a chronic disease that involves declines in cognitive and functional status. Care for individuals with dementia involves both health and social care and, perhaps more than other conditions, substantial amounts of care from informal caregivers. The burden of dementia on health and social care systems and, through informal care giving, on labour markets is a profound public policy challenge. Linking broad and deep data will allow governments, industry and other key stakeholders to co-operate in a way that generates evidence about the social and economic impacts of dementia in order to advance policies and services that best serve citizens, shareholders, individuals with dementia and their loved ones and caregivers.

There are many ongoing international efforts in place to address the dementia challenge and the Toronto workshop was designed to build on and support those efforts. The workshop attracted over 60 individuals from across the world to hear presentations by the authors of the workshop papers, to listen to updates from other initiatives and to discuss the role that linking broad and deep data could have in supporting and building on those efforts. The next section of this chapter provides a summary of the key themes of the workshop followed by conclusions and potential actions to make broad and deep data a resource for dementia care and cure.

The full text of the papers drafted by workshop speakers to support the discussions are each included as chapters of this report and the agenda for the meeting and the list of attendees is provided in Annex A.

1.1. What are the opportunities and challenges in linking broad and deep data?

The value of bringing together broad data on exposures, outcomes and health care utilisation together with deep clinical and biological data lies in the creation of a resource that will allow scientists from different disciplines to work together to create new insights that will support both cure and care. For example, when deep data about genetic profiles can be combined with broad data about health care treatments it is possible to identify very specific types of patients that benefit most from particular treatment regimes. This session provided perspectives from government, researchers, industry, foundations and patient groups on the opportunities that could be provided by efforts to link broad and deep data and the challenges that need to be faced.

Governments' approach to dementia cannot rely on the thinking that has been typically used to address acute health care problems. There are opportunities for government to work in five broad areas – health policy, including improved integrated care across the life course; economic policy, such as reducing productivity impacts and ensuring fair treatment of caregivers; and research and innovation, including improving care and searching for a cure; supporting caregivers; and raising public awareness. The common elements across these five areas are that they all create and rely on data and there needs to be cross-sectorial action.

Governments can play an important role in efforts to create big data resources through their regulatory and legislative roles related to privacy, data access, and data standardisation; through their role as a provider and funder of health and social services; and as the largest supporters of research. Governments can also improve data in order to meet broader social and economic policy objectives. Governments need to be clear about the importance of big data; expand and support the organisation of data to reflect the fact that care for dementia extends beyond the traditional boundaries of health care services;

and ensure that big data are used across health, social care, and research sectors to their greatest advantage.

Linking broad and deep data could be useful for advancing our understanding of disease progression and of the complex interplay between genes and the environment. Proof of principle studies in these two areas could be pursued. In terms of the current situation, although there are many important biological, clinical and population data sets available, key challenges that would first need to be addressed before reaping the benefits of linked data include making existing and newly acquired data available in open access platforms that protect participants' privacy; harmonising data so that they can be usefully merged; improving our collection of population-based exposure data; curating data bases; and managing expectations. Appropriate funding needs to be set aside for all phases of a big data discovery paradigm as part of a balanced portfolio of research.

Drug discovery and development rely on biochemical or phenotypic characterisation. There are opportunities and challenges in both approaches. The creation of an accessible big data resource for dementia could provide a "base camp" to support a range of efforts including opportunities around disease categorisation, therapies for vascular dementia, disease modifying drugs, symptomatic therapies and preventive and risk-modifying strategies. Bringing broad and deep data together can help to provide a better understanding of disease categories and progression that will allow for more focused efforts around cardiovascular medicines and symptomatic treatments. Inclusion of data on exposures and risk factors will allow for preventive therapies and non-pharmaceutical approaches to risk-factor modification. Better accounting of the full range of costs of dementia will clarify the rate of return on new interventions and spur investment in research and discovery.

Key conclusions included the importance of:

- Protecting privacy and enabling access to data by including the perspectives of patients – the individuals who provide the data and whose privacy requires protection – and researchers – the individuals who need access to data for research that leads to impactful outcomes, including publications, commercialisation, and knowledge translation tools .
    - Focusing on the quality of data, developing standards, and recognising that some data sources are inherently less accurate than others and that knowledge of variation in quality is essential in developing and using linked data.
    - Developing new approaches to analytics and the recognition that data mining and machine learning can provide new insights, including tools to discover the "unexpected"; as well as developing a greater capacity to undertake big data analytics that can be applied to linked data that are unique to dementia.
    - Understanding and considering patient and caregiver expectations including involving the public in discussions about the secondary use of health data to improve dementia cure and care and the data governance in place to safeguard the privacy of patients' whose data are to be studied.

1.2. Are the data available and useable?

It will be challenging to create a big data resource that brings different data sources together that can be shared internationally. This effort needs to be guided by principles that ensure the integrity, excellence and multi-disciplinary nature of the science, while at the same recognising the importance of privacy and data security. Moving forward requires understanding the "how" of linked big data, such as where should the analysis occur and does the data need to be centralised to be linked? Current efforts to create large linked data with over 100 000 individuals within broad data and tens of thousands within deep data are starting to provide some answers.

The experience of the Ontario Brain Institute (OBI) in its Brain-CODE initiative suggests that putting the patient at the centre of the data development project and creating partnerships among all key stakeholders are essential first steps in a process that recognises the value of mutual learning on data governance and standardisation policies. There is a need to have an open dialogue among existing big data initiatives, to develop a shared commitment to privacy by design, and to embark on specific efforts to test the feasibility and sustainability of international data sharing.

The G8 countries commitment to dementia cure and care provides an impetus for improving the environment for international research co-operation. This effort involves working with the OECD on taking stock of the current national incentive structures for research and considering changes that could promote and accelerate discovery and support transformation and innovation in care. Strategic priority areas should be identified including collaboration among big data initiatives, public private partnerships, and open science principles for greater international collaboration.

There are technical challenges around big data management and analytics and organisational challenges around governance, sustainability, security and access to data. The OECD is investigating a specific set of case studies with the Oxford Internet Institute in the United Kingdom. Preliminary findings from a case study of the Alzheimer's Disease Neuroimaging Initiative (ADNI) showed that ADNI had been successful in creating a model for widespread data sharing that has grown into a world-wide effort. Contributions of ADNI that were highlighted included its model of data sharing without embargo and its role in standardising methods and measures for clinical trials. In general, strategies to accelerate dementia research in the next five years should include changing mindsets around sharing data, attracting sufficient bioinformatics talent, supporting policies around collaboration and introducing uniform patient consent and models for re-use of data.

Key conclusions were:

- The value of linking broad and deep data is predicated on sharing data and creating a culture of open science.
- There needs to be a concerted effort to address issues that limit data sharing between scientists and research groups.
- Patients could be important advocates in creating pressure for more open-access data as they have provided the data and would benefit from a greater use of the data to increase the possibility of successful discoveries.
- There also needs to be a structured set of incentives that would allow for partnerships between the public and private sectors.
- Case studies are useful and efforts to develop some specific real-world examples of linking broad and deep data could provide proof of the benefits of scientific and data sharing principles.

1.3. What will be the best way to build trust?

Linking data is the key to discovery and research but, to enable such links, data privacy and trust in data holders and researchers is crucial. Best practices in the protection of data subjects' privacy, in the governance of data by national authorities and in the use of data to measure health system performance must be understood and applied.

The key principles in privacy by design include proactive not reactive privacy protection so that privacy protection is the default setting. This includes privacy embedded in design, end-to-end security, and visibility and transparency of data privacy protections. The privacy-by-design method is increasingly being adopted internationally and has been used to support big data initiatives in many jurisdictions including Ontario in Canada (Cavoukian, 2014).

Data that describes health care pathways and outcomes is a key element of the broad data that needs to be part of an international strategy around big data and dementia. Broad data often requires linkage of data sets within and across sectors. Effective collaboration between health ministries, social care ministries, justice ministries and data privacy regulators is essential if governments are to evolve toward a health data governance framework where societal benefits from personal health data use are maximised and risks to individuals from data use are minimised. Only half of recently surveyed OECD countries are engaged regularly in data linkage studies to monitor health care quality and about half are beginning to use data from electronic health records for national health and health care monitoring.

The OECD is identifying best practices in data governance that are central to privacy-protective uses of broad data. Key elements of data governance frameworks include public consultation and information about the collection and use of personal health data and the safeguards applied; legislation that enables data sharing and use, subject to suitable safeguards; data processors that are held to high standards for data governance; data-use approval processes that are fair and transparent; and use of best practices in data de-identification and secure data access. The study also identified areas that would benefit from further international collaboration including supporting multi-country data sharing projects by comparing national privacy laws to determine which laws offer similar and adequate protection; developing an international consensus on norms for the accreditation or certification of data processors; and developing a shared view of fair and practical approaches to obtaining consent for uses of patients' data within broad datasets. Mechanisms are needed to engage the public in the discussion about benefits of these data and the commitment to data privacy and the rights of data subjects.

Key conclusions were that:

- Privacy is a central issue and the privacy by design model highlights the need to build privacy protection into all steps and to recognise that privacy is not something that is added on after data systems are already implemented.
- The notion that privacy can never be absolutely guaranteed raises the importance of actively involving the public in a discussion about the benefits and risks of data use and the safeguards in place to mitigate those risks.
- If the public agree that linked data have the potential to improve both cure research and care delivery, they will be more likely to recognise due diligence efforts to protect privacy.

- New dynamic models of patient consent to make data available for future research, subject to safeguards, are needed.
- Campaigns that ask individuals to "donate their data" are strategies to improve public awareness of the benefits of data use, the safeguards and their rights.

1.4. How can we benchmark performance to make progress in dementia care?

Governments face the daunting public policy challenge of dealing with the large and growing burden of dementia. High quality and sustainable systems of care for dementia will require innovation and profound changes in financing and health and social care delivery mechanisms. International performance measurement and practice benchmarking systems will be fundamental. Such measures enable governments to implement sound public policy informed by shared learning from successful policy innovations. A first step would be a conceptual framework for performance measurement of dementia care systems that can be used to map current performance comparison efforts, define gaps and strengthen health information systems to fill performance measurement gaps. The World Health Organization (WHO) and the OECD could engage their member countries in a co-ordinated and collaborative effort to share best practices through a focused practice benchmarking effort for dementia care that reflects national dementia care strategies and current policy dilemmas. Performance comparisons should be systematic and supported by relevant and valid information that are interpreted in context. Practice benchmarking for dementia care systems will require substantial investments.

Key conclusions were that:

- Developing comparable health system performance indicators and projections of the costs of dementia care could be powerful tools for increasing government support of research on dementia care and cure.
- Context and cultural norms should be understood and taken into account when assessing and comparing performance of dementia care systems, including looking into the role caregivers play in care delivery systems in various contexts.

1.5. Data-driven health innovation: Next steps for Canada, the OECD, and the world

Making progress on the big data and dementia agenda will involve different actors moving on multiple fronts. The OECD and other organisations such as the World Health Organization (WHO) are willing to facilitate international co-operation and support efforts to share best practices and develop guidelines. The OECD has a rich history of supporting both scientific collaboration and efforts around health and social care system performance and benchmarking.

National governments, however, have a much more direct role to play in advancing dementia research and care by setting policy frameworks; legislating and regulating data privacy and access; and funding health research and health and social care systems.

Moving forward will require active involvement of the research community, the private sector and the public. Researchers and research institutions will need to explore ways to better share ideas and to create partnerships. Creating a culture of open science will require understanding and addressing the concerns of scientists and partnering with the institutions that employ and support researchers. There is also an important role for businesses and the private sector. This will include the pharmaceutical industry but also broader private sector interests in health and social care. In the context of big data, private sector involvement should also include the large number of companies and businesses that are involved in the production and analysis of large data. Finally, but perhaps most importantly, is the involvement of the public in strategies to enable data to support research and care. Dementia is a condition that does not just affect patients but also their families and caregivers and ultimately, given its scope, economies and the social fabric. Engaging the public in understanding the potential value of linking data and the balance between that and legitimate and fundamental concerns about privacy is essential to moving forward.

There is potential in linking broad and deep data and work in this area could help drive both discovery research and care improvement. To realise this potential, financial and organisational challenges and concerns about the protection of data privacy must be addressed. The way forward could involve creating strategies for global co-operation in defining shared policy challenges and best practices and at the same time building on existing data projects and working on specific proof of principle projects to better understand the approaches to linking broad and deep data and the value of such efforts.

Producing, linking and analysing data is costly and an effort is needed to more clearly identify the real value of data development in order to obtain support from both the private and public sectors. A business case for public-sector support could include making an argument to finance ministries that a growing burden of dementia will have a substantial impact on economies and labour markets. Private sector support will require clear opportunities for commercial benefit.

There was also agreement that a better articulation of the benefits from linking broad and deep data would be essential to a balanced discussion of the risks of data use and safeguards to address data privacy concerns. A key step would be a systematic effort to explain to the public the benefits of donating or allowing access to data for linkage. This could build on existing models of organ or tissue donation that recognise both the risks and the benefits. Public dialogue must be supported by effective data governance strategies, developed by governments and regulators, that provide protections and oversight of data linkage and data access efforts. This should include legislation on data sharing and use, public consultation, data-use approval processes that are fair and transparent to the public and use of best practices in data de-identification and secure data access. The notion of Privacy by Design, in which privacy is built in from the outset and is paramount at all stages, could be useful in this context. This commitment to standards and processes should be buttressed by stiff penalties for misuse of data. The public needs to be convinced that the risks to privacy from data linkage for research will be minimised and that these risks are far outweighed by the benefits. This again argues for the importance of showing the value of data linkage in proof of principle projects before committing to large scale investments and potentially politically contentious efforts to create large accessible international big data resources.

A comprehensive strategy that creates an infrastructure that supports efforts to link broad and deep data in all interested countries is needed. The strategy should encourage specific collaborative efforts that can better define the value of broad and deep data linkage. This work will build and support existing efforts around discovery research in dementia and will help to ensure that there are international and national efforts focused on performance measurement and supporting improvement in systems of health and social care for all those affected by dementia.

Key next steps that emerged from the meeting included:

- Pursue the possibility to develop an international centre of excellence or a clearing house to discuss issues around good practice in data governance, privacy protection and data standards to support national development of broad and deep data and to support multi-country projects involving data sharing.
- Develop international benchmarks and comparisons of the performance of health systems in caring for dementia patients, starting with the identification of key performance measures, and then investigating and comparing data sources, developing internationally comparable definitions and piloting indicator development.
- Pursue an international project involving the linkage of broad and deep data as a pilot or proof of concept study to demonstrate the benefits of this type of data to dementia research and care and as a test bed to work through challenges and develop solutions for future projects.

With appropriate support, these steps could enable a leap forward in research innovation and monitoring to improve diagnosis, treatment and continue efforts to find a cure; to enhance the quality of life of patients and their families; and to support more efficient use of health care resources and more positive labour market and economic outcomes.

Note

1. This chapter has been written by Geoffrey Anderson, PhD, Institute of Health Policy, Management and Evaluation, University of Toronto, Canada; Adalsteinn Brown, PhD, Institute of Health Policy, Management and Evaluation, University of Toronto, Canada; Francesca Colombo, MSc; OECD; Jillian Oderkirk, MA, OECD; Elettra Ronchi, PhD, OECD; Donald T. Stuss, PhD, Ontario Brain Institute, Toronto, Canada; Jeremy Veillard, PhD, Canadian Institute for Health Information, Toronto.

References

Cavoukian, A (2014), 'Privacy-by-Design: Seven Foundational Principles', www.privacybydesign.ca/index.php/about-pbd/7-foundational-principles/ accessed 27 November 2014.

G8 Dementia Summit Communiqué (2013), www.gov.uk/government/uploads/system/uploads/attachment_data/file/265868/2901669_G8_DementiaSummitCommunique_acc.pdf accessed 27 November 2014.

OECD (2015), *Data-Driven Innovation for Growth and Well-Being*, OECD Publishing, Paris, forthcoming.

OECD (2014), "Unleashing the Power of Big Data for Alzheimer's Disease and Dementia Research: Main Points of the OECD Expert Consultation on Unlocking Global Collaboration to Accelerate Innovation for Alzheimer's Disease and Dementia", *OECD Digital Economy Papers*, No. 233, OECD Publishing, Paris, http://dx.doi.org/10.1787/5jz73kvmvbwb-en.

Chapter 2

The critical and complex challenge of dementia: Why governments must use big data to respond to the challenges of dementia

Natalie Warrick, Adalsteinn Brown and Kirk Nylen[1]

Dementia is a global challenge to all levels of government in every country. Many governments have developed policy frameworks to deal with the dementia challenge and these policies deal with issues related to the care for those with dementia and their caregivers, as well as support for efforts to identify strategies for prevention and cure. Governments can play an important role in efforts to create big data resources through their regulatory and legislative roles related to privacy, data access, data standardisation, and broader economic and trade policy, through their role as a provider and funder of health and social services, and as the largest supporters of research. Governments need to be clear around the importance of big data, expand and support the organisation of data to reflect the fact that care for dementia is bigger than just health care services, and ensure that big data are used across our health, social care, and research sectors to their greatest advantage.

2.1. The challenge

Dementia, a group of neurodegenerative disorders characterised by a progressive and premature decline in cognitive ability such as Alzheimer's disease, currently affects more than 35 million individuals worldwide. Without any change in prevention or cure, this number will likely double every 20 years with an estimated 115 million cases by 2050 (Prince et al., 2013). These projections are likely low given current levels of under- and late diagnosis of dementia.

Dementia is one of the greatest challenges to health system sustainability. Individuals with dementia are identified and treated by providers across the health care system with the most severe cases often requiring residential care. It is a chronic disease, often accompanied by other chronic diseases making the treatment of dementia and the other diseases more complicated. Like other chronic diseases, efforts to reduce the risk and progression of dementia through healthy behaviours rely on the same health care, public health, and educational efforts. But dementia is also a significant social policy challenge. An overwhelming amount of the care for individuals with dementia takes place in the informal care system and is provided by family and friends who face significant health risks due to the burden of caregiving as well as economic loss and social isolation because of the time required to provide care. Perhaps most challenging is the fact that the fastest growth in the prevalence of dementia is in low- and middle-income countries, where the social and health care infrastructure may be the least developed, further re-enforcing inequities within those countries and with high-income countries.

2.2. Government responses to the challenge

Recognising the challenges posed by dementia, a number of countries and even regions have begun developing plans and mobilising resources to meet these challenges. The role of government will be pivotal in developing and implementing measures to reduce the growth in dementia, ensure high quality care for dementia, control expenditures on dementia, and support individuals with dementia and their caregivers against social and economic hardship. In this regard, dementia is typical of the worldwide epidemic of chronic disease that threatens the sustainability of health and social care systems and has a huge impact on economic productivity. However, dementia may reflect the most complex chronic disease challenge. The intersection of dementia's high and growing prevalence, the way that dementia reduces the independence of those with the disease, and the overall ageing of the population (including the most likely caregivers of persons with dementia) means that relatively simple and commonly used health care policies such as increased compliance to guidelines for dementia care or new screening and early detection programmes, although helpful, will provide little reduction in the impact of dementia by themselves. Substitution of care across formal and informal (Stabile et al., 2006) and acute and community-based sectors is also likely taking place, further emphasizing the importance of carefully balancing formal and informal resources[2] in diseases like dementia.

The challenge of dementia is further complicated by the fact that the way various health, social care, and economic policies interact to support people with dementia and their caregivers is poorly understood and likely dependent on national and local context. When the economic picture is refocused on the individual, the costs of caring for someone with dementia include lost income, lower mobility, higher direct health care costs, and lower labour market participation. Given that the majority of caregivers are women, economic and labour market policy issues also include issues of equity. The challenge to typical policy making is the close relationship between broader trends in health care, health care for dementia, social care and support for those caring for someone with dementia, and economic and labour market policy making it difficult to isolate or target one area for policy intervention. Furthermore, this intersection of health care, social services, economic, and employment policy typically involves multiple levels of government within each country, further complicating policy development and implementation.

Given the size and complexity of the dementia challenge, it is not surprising that governments are engaged in different combinations of policies (Table 2.1). The current range of polices addressing dementia is wide and touches on issues ranging from genetic counseling through to tax credits. Although there is no common template for dementia plans, there are elements that are common to many plans that spread across health care and other policy areas including: a) earlier detection and treatment; b) improved training for clinicians in diagnosis and care; c) increased respite care; d) help for caregivers including system navigation and caregiver needs assessment; e) financial support for caregivers; and f) increased education about the disease and co-ordination services across health and social care. However, it is clear that there is no single appropriate approach to the disease, nor that any of the current approaches to dementia are adequate or effective.

As much as health care programmes targeted at dementia vary across countries, caregiver support initiatives vary at least as much. Evidence suggests that financial support to caregivers can help sustain them in their role and lead to better outcomes for the recipients of their care (Fujisawa and Colombo, 2009). The extent of such supports varies across the OECD with different countries adopting similar, though not consistent, allocation mechanisms, which can include care allowances, tax exemptions or contributions to pension schemes. Interventions for caregivers can extend to labour policy with some countries experimenting with tax credits, labour market interventions, and direct income supports. Other emerging policy issues such as co-operative care models, long-term care insurance and direct funding to caregivers may provide opportunities for persons with dementia and their caregivers, but their relative effectiveness is not known. Even where there are common policies such as respite care or care-leave arrangements, these can vary substantially across countries in nature, length and total amount of compensation without clear evidence for greater or less support. For example, the National Respite for Carers Program in Australia provides caregivers access to respite and a direct allowance. The United Kingdom, which in 2004 passed the *Carers Equal Opportunities Act*, supports unpaid care through employment opportunities, extended benefits, and additional economic supports. Low-income caregivers in Germany are provided periods of respite and are able to take advantage of Social Long-Term Care Insurance benefits, essentially providing full pay during a leave of absence to perform caregiving duties. Provinces across Canada are using respite, counseling and peer support, and economic benefits such as pension support.

Perhaps the strongest argument in favour of a strong role for governments in dementia policy related to big data is the interconnectedness of health care, social care, labour, and economic policy in dementia. Only governments are capable of co-ordinating and aligning the different policy areas that require attention in the case of dementia and thus are likely the most immediate users and beneficiaries of more useful data on dementia. However, another strong argument is the importance of developing cures and caring strategies (research) for dementia through big data, which will also require government leadership. In the following sections, we outline why it is that governments need to prioritise the use of big data in dementia research, planning, and performance management (Table 2.2).

Table 2.1. Common policy elements from worldwide Alzheimer's disease and dementia plans

	Australia	England	Finland	France	Ireland	Israel	Japan	Netherlands	Norway	Scotland	United States	Luxembourg	Switzerland	Wales	Republic of Korea
1. Awareness raising	Yes	Yes	Yes	Yes	Yes	Yes	Yes		Yes		Yes	Yes	Yes	Yes	Yes
2. Dementia training	Yes	Yes		Yes	Yes	Yes			Yes	Yes		Yes	Yes	Yes	Yes
3. Diagnosis	Yes	Yes			Yes	Yes	Yes	Yes	Yes	Yes		Yes			Yes
4. Risk factors, prevention and access to treatment	Yes	Yes			Yes	Yes	Yes		Yes		Yes	Yes		Yes	
5. Care co-ordination	Yes	Yes				Yes	Yes	Yes		Yes					
6. Changes in physician practice/ procedure	Yes	Yes	Yes	Yes		Yes			Yes	Yes		Yes			
7. Quality care recommendation	Yes	Yes		Yes	Yes			Yes	Yes	Yes	Yes		Yes		
8. Legal ethical issues/rights	Yes				Yes	Yes			Yes	Yes					
9. Improved data	Yes										Yes		Yes		
10. Research funding	Yes	Yes	Yes	Yes	Yes	Yes			Yes					Yes	
11. Family caregiver supports, assessment and/or funding		Yes	Yes	Yes	Yes	Yes	Yes	Yes	Yes		Yes				Yes
12. Policy office and intergovernmental policies	Yes	Yes							Yes		Yes				

Source: Alzheimer Disease International (2014), "Government Alzheimer Plans", Alzheimer's Disease International, London, Retrieved from www.alz.co.uk/alzheimer-plans.

2.3. Opportunities for government to support the creation of better big data

Big data have been inconsistently defined. This is not surprising given the challenges posed by big data. As indicated in the 2014 OECD report on harnessing big data, "big data is not just a quantitative change, it is a conceptual and methodological change" (p. 18). One possible definition fitting with the previous statement is that big data are "data whose size forces us to look beyond the tried-and-true methods that are prevalent" (Jacobs, 2009, p. 11). Though this definition seems to imply the notion that new methods will always be on the horizon – and by extension that the definition of big data will also change over time – it also suggests that current strategies for managing data are insufficient to cope with big data.

The ability to use big data (broad transactional or administrative data sets and deep detailed clinical and biologic data sets) to predict and prevent, detect (earlier), mitigate risk, care better for, and even cure dementia depends on the ability to organise, link, and share data. Advances in research technology (e.g., molecular assays, DNA sequencing and other high-throughput technologies) as well as a steep drop in costs associated with these technologies have advanced research, generating greater volumes of data at a faster rate. This argument for the importance of big data to identify cures and support better care for dementia patients is likely well accepted. However, the interconnectedness of the policy issues in dementia means that dementia problems can only be fully understood by examining data from multiple data sources that are rarely linked together and usually administered or overseen by different parts of government, further emphasizing the importance and challenges associated with big data related to dementia. However, all of these data must be turned into knowledge.

A 2014 OECD report on big data in health care noted that in order to inform policy making regarding cure and care, researchers and policy makers must have three types of knowledge about dementia:

- knowledge from research – "evidence-based care" (p. 6)
- knowledge from analysis of routinely collected or audit data "statistics" or "information" (pp. 10, 18)
- knowledge harvested from the patient experience (p. 18).

However, as noted above, the scope of services relevant to dementia patients and their caregivers goes well beyond these sources of data. Indeed, the importance of data across the spectrum of government funded or regulated services suggests the first opportunity for government involvement is to support the collection of data across all of the touch points where dementia patients or their caregivers deal with health, social, and economic policy related services. Governments at every level (national, regional, and municipal) are the only ones that can attach data collection requirements to these services. Augmenting these services with data collection (Parmar et al., 2014, address this issue from a private sector perspective in a recent Harvard Business Review on the role of big data in driving innovation) and perhaps data sharing or communication can help collect and make better use of data that can improve dementia care and services.

At the same time, these data and the resulting knowledge must be used to have impact on dementia. Improving care and support of persons with dementia and their caregivers requires a health system populated with administrators and clinicians who can integrate all three types of knowledge. As noted in the same OECD report, "No one nation, agency, institution, company or industry has all the assets to pursue this type of research independently" (OECD, 2014, p. 31). This means that big data strategies should also look at how resources can be integrated and shared both within and between countries to allow for optimal co-ordination of data and knowledge, again requiring government intervention. Another key area for government involvement is exploration and better understanding of how assets like data can or should be profitably shared among different actors with the goal of improving care and the potential for a cure. This area of action can extend to international action plans among governments, industry or non-profit organisations like Alzheimer societies.

Such international activity may in turn help stimulate more national level activity given that only 15 out of 193 WHO countries have established national dementia plans (Prince et al., 2013) and only three plans (Australia, the United States, and Switzerland) explicitly acknowledge the need for better data or data sharing. Future international plans may usefully focus on how to co-ordinate data collection and storage efforts and provide frameworks for sharing and valuing data among countries to maximise the use of data while minimising risk and unnecessary duplication. Moreover, owing to the rapid increases in dementia prevalence across low-income countries, governments focused on global health may also work towards effective knowledge transfer about opportunities to improve care in developing countries where dementia rates are also substantially rising or where public knowledge of dementia care models may be low (Suzuki et al., 2014). Expansion of Alzheimer's Disease International's "Helping Carers to Care Intervention", a randomised controlled trial of education and training of caregivers with proven impact on caregivers, has also proven to be particularly effective in low and middle-income countries (ADI, 2014b).

Success in using big data will require more than just international co-operation. Three key issues surrounding big data have been previously identified. The first of these is volume, that is, the sheer mass of data that are being generated by machines on networks and through human interaction via social media are contributing to the growing costs of data storage, privacy compliance, and capacity to interpret for health and social service organisations. The costs of linking, organising, and analysing data require considerable investment and collaboration that can only come from government in most cases (OECD, 2014). The second issue is the variety of data that have been collected and the variation in collection systems. Minimum data specifications, such as diagnosis classification systems can lead to data inconsistencies. The third issue is one of velocity. The pace at which data are collected is contributing to the obsolescence of traditional database management systems (OECD, 2014).

The inability to address adequately these issues is not surprising. Comparability of the content of the data collected across databases often must be reconciled with use of common data elements where possible. Agreement on epidemiological, bioinformatics, and statistical methods to overcome differences in study design, number of participants, participant recruitment, number and type of biological samples collected, remains elusive in dementia as in most other areas. Governments have already invested in many large, population-based studies. Harmonising and pooling of these databases is important for the same reasons that justified the earlier large studies including:

- larger sample sizes
- greater generalisability of studies
- improved validity of comparative research

- more efficient secondary use of existing data
- greater opportunities for collaboration and multi-centre research
- stronger research on the interactions of different diseases (e.g., relationship to other disorders; impact across sectors) (Doiron et al., 2013).

However, harmonisation of all data elements may be impossible, so co-operation across researchers and across countries may also look profitably to harmonisation of routinely collected data on dementia and to methods of matching comparable data sources where they exist.

Another critical problem facing international data sharing and linkage is the absence of standardised platforms for sharing information (OECD, 2014). In particular, the lack of a shared platform for metrics of biomarkers and dementia is made more problematic due to the fact that people with signs and symptoms are usually diagnosed based on crude behavioural endpoints (e.g., abnormal memory loss). New research has shown that there are multiple causes of dementia. Researchers have yet to reach a consensus on the already identified early biomarkers of dementia (e.g., energy metabolism disease, vascular pathology, genetics, epigenetics, etc.). Countries could establish an international peer review board to advance policies that support a registry to streamline clinical trials. These challenges are mirrored by challenges in the inconsistent coding of dementia in routinely collected health care data, inconsistent diagnosis or case-finding protocols, and different definitions necessary to qualify for benefits. All of these variations reduce the within-dataset utility of information on dementia and the ability to link across data sets and data across countries. Again, this sort of activity will require government involvement and support of data sharing and standardisation activities.

2.4. Privacy and confidentiality

Health and other information on individuals that are held by governments are a lightning rod for controversy. However, modern encryption techniques, such as those used by banks for internet banking, as well as transparent consent procedures have been used by virtually all studies on dementia and are supported by modern ethics review boards. However, maintaining confidentiality and privacy requires government intervention. International data sharing agreements can help to facilitate the exchange of data while maintaining privacy and confidentiality; but in order to realise the greatest value from big data, it may be useful to consider open source approaches to data management as they represent one possible solution to the questions and problems surrounding intellectual property (OECD, 2014). Open source describes a set of rules and practices for defining a community of developers through which information is freely disclosed and distributed (Auyoung et al., 2007). Another useful strategy to resolve ethico-legal constraints is pooled analysis of individual-level data, which can be achieved without sharing data about individuals in any given jurisdiction using different methods (i.e. Doiron et al., 2013; Fortier et al., 2011). These sorts of shifts in policy will likely require a central, government-mandated approach if they are to be tested and spread quickly if found to be effective.

The collection of big data does create real risks for individuals around insurance and employment. Employers and insurers may be cautious about hiring or covering individuals at risk for dementia. Genetic information non-discrimination and its associated acts in the United States and a number of European countries (NIH, 2012) ban employers and health insurers from denying coverage or increasing premiums on healthy persons who have a known genetic predisposition to developing a disease in the future. International or broadly held standards that prevent genetic discrimination should increase participation of persons with or at risk of dementia, and their caregivers in big data efforts, and the value of sharing these data.

2.5. Support for research data collection and the capacity to use data

Fundamentally, big data will benefit the fight against dementia in two ways. First, it will create the data sets that can accelerate the development and testing of cures for different dementias. Second, it can create the knowledge – whether it is evidence on what care pathways work, information on how different providers perform, or advice on what coping strategies have worked for different groups of caregivers – that can support a better dementia care system. In the first instance, the faster pursuit of cures, government intervention is focused on questions around how best to collect data in a co-ordinated way across settings and in concert with other jurisdictions. In the second instance – the improvement of formal and informal care systems – government intervention goes well beyond the data themselves.

Government activities to standardise and make data on dementia safe are critical to the value of big data, but the most significant contribution of governments may be to the political and policy context around the collection and use of these data. For example, governments can use their research funding bodies to prioritise dementia research and ensure that applicants create plans to work collaboratively and collect data in a manner that is consistent with other international groups. Groups such as the NIH have done considerable work around establishing common data elements, which others can use to ensure that data collection is standardised. In this way, governments can marshal dementia researchers and resources to ensure comparability, co-ordination and integration of research efforts across regions so that data and knowledge can be shared internationally.

A concept discussed in detail by Stuss et al. (in this series) is "deep and broad" data. Deep data refer to in-depth research data on individuals. Broad data refer to transactional or health system utilisation data. Combining these types of data will enable a new type of research that can transform our understanding of dementia and how to mobilise resources around it. Government has two key roles in enabling the use of broad and deep data. The first is discussed above, that is, prioritising dementia research to develop a rich source of "deep data". The second is to facilitate access to broad data for research, evaluation, and performance management purposes in an accessible yet secure environment particularly if it supports the routine collection of more transactional data as suggested above.

Public opinion on the use of data is challenging. Although the public generally are cautious about the use of their data, they are also supportive of the use of data to support better care and faster cures. Not surprisingly, privacy legislation around health data in many countries both creates protections against the disclosure of data, while trying to create safe contexts in which these data may be used. This is complicated by the fact that the public often has little knowledge about how health research is conducted (Cameron, 2013). Although every country will strike a different balance between use of data and protection of privacy, only government can strike this balance.

At the same time, the use of data by the health care systems is challenging. The volume of data created every day in the health system would overwhelm even the most sophisticated administrators without dramatic increases in the technological capacity and managerial insight into these data. Most governments have made strategic investments in the infrastructure to collect data on health care. Still, reaping value from these data will require further investments that facilitate the ability to link, analyse, and use these data in decision making.

Data rarely drive change on their own, rather they must be linked to decisions about resource allocation at every level of the system and supported by decision aids and the capacity to continuously analyse data. In turn, this supports governments in finding answers to complex social problems (e.g., Do we build more long-term care homes? Do we reprioritise hospital wards to day hospitals for dementia? Do we introduce dementia screening into the primary care visit protocol for seniors? Do we change tax credit levels or provide pension support for dementia caregivers?). As we learn more about how to best care for and support people with dementia and their caregivers, we become responsible for translating this information into tools and policies that support better decisions. These tools can be educational programmes for the public and providers, decision-support aids, and even performance measurement and management techniques.

Big data insights may also stimulate the development of new policies that have implications beyond dementia care such as those that support customised balancing of support for formal and informal care, plans for the redevelopment of long-term care infrastructure, and even tax policy. Within the health care system, they will also require the examination of a range of policies around reimbursement and oversight to ensure that these existing policies do not inappropriately limit new practices that can improve care. In addition to support for data collection and organisation, governments may want to invest in training programmes and set standards that support the integration of big data into decision making where possible at the policy, administrative, and even clinical decision-making levels. Again, these are activities that only government can undertake with any speed.

Finally, the burden of care for people with dementia often rests with informal family caregivers, most of whom are unpaid (Keefe et al., 2011). Within most health systems it is the care recipients and not the caregivers who are formally acknowledged as requiring support. This in turn has consequences for the sustainability of care models. The development of support policy for informal caregivers has been suggested as one means of preventing the steep declines in anticipated informal caregiving capacity that has been projected to increase system costs by 5% to 35% (OECD, 2011). However, all governments will need to consider explicitly if and how they expand their notion of the health care system beyond regulated care providers to include informal caregivers.

2.6. Research policy and dementia

The growth of big data will impact research policy. Governments have the opportunity to create dedicated funding streams to attract and retain PhD students, early career researchers, and public health and health administrators to learn strategies for collaboration and use of large datasets. They may also support methodological research to create the new tools necessary to use big (broad and deep) data studies to understand dementia, for example by comparing findings from genetics with brain imaging results (Scott et al., 2013). Similarly, governments can attract researchers by making available these sorts of broad and deep data for these studies through research funding requirements or other mechanisms. The process of accessing data is currently often cumbersome and challenging, deterring most researchers. The development of a resource (toolkit, online modules, etc.) and/or specialised training programme for researchers and scientists would also expand the capacity of researchers. As part of skill building, governments could partner with both industry and academia to host annual competitions for early careerist scientists, undergraduate and graduate students to use big data in pursuit and development of the next wave of scientists.

The 2014 OECD report on big data argued that policy makers should also be interested in harnessing the unused worldwide potential to analyse large repositories of data and engage the public through the use of citizen science. Citizen science describes the involvement of non-professionals in processing data through crowdsourcing, and mass-participation to generate, collect, and analyse data. Governments and their agencies may find these relatively low-cost means of leveraging the capacity and data attractive. Given that governments everywhere are engaging the public through social media, these interactions may offer new opportunities to further data collection and awareness and take advantage of innovations such as time-banking.

Despite strong efforts in many countries to support dementia research, there remains a large gap between our understanding of the many factors implicated in dementia and how health care is organised and delivered. Vast amounts of information about individuals (e.g., genetics, imaging, etc.) and their environments are being assembled into "big data" sets for the first time with opportunities to conduct research and support public policy decision making never before possible. Big data has the potential to transform dementia prevention, early detection, cure and care, but a number of barriers have already been identified. There are three components about shifting upstream but such transformation will also require a better understanding of more general health services research topics such as prevention and case finding, shifting care into community settings, and the more effective support and engagement of care givers.

New internet networking technologies and database management systems are providing the means to support collaborative, multi-centre research that adds value to big data analyses, as well as making it more secure. These technologies and systems are:

- Transforming existing data collected by different studies into a common format through the use of processing algorithms.
- Interconnecting harmonised databases located across political jurisdictions via federated web-based infrastructure.
- Achieving joint statistical analyses of harmonised datasets without pooling or sharing individual-level data (Doiron et al., 2013).

2.7. Moving forward

No cure for dementia currently exists. After expenditures of billions of dollars on new drugs, presently only four drugs provide modest symptomatic relief over six to eighteen months and they do not slow down the progression of the disease (Lin et al., 2013). Recent models relate Alzheimer's disease to diabetes, midlife hypertension, midlife obesity, smoking, depression, cognitive inactivity/low educational attainment and physical inactivity (Barnes and Yaffe, 2011). A relative reduction of 10% each decade in all seven of these potentially modifiable risk factors could reduce the number of cases of Alzheimer's disease in 2050 by 8.3% (Norton et al., 2014). Lifestyle, pharmacologic or care practice interventions that delay onset of dementia may offer the best near-term chance for responding to the "grand global challenge" in health care including dementia

(OECD, 2014). However, the capacity to detect/diagnose and treat dementia remains limited and research has not yet provided much guidance.

Governments can create, organise, and leverage existing big data assets in the fight against dementia. The first major area of action relates to government's role as a major funder or provider of health and social care services. Governments at all levels can ensure that data are collected at each point where dementia patients and their caregivers touch the health and social care systems. They can organise, share, utilise and link these data to economic and other sources of data. In most cases, only governments have the scope and opportunity to pursue these strategies. Continuing along this value chain, governments can support capacity development and set standards to make sure that these data and resulting insights are used to their full potential to make better decisions on policy, for performance management, and to guide clinical decision making and other decisions by clinicians, dementia patients and their caregivers. There are a variety of novel ways in which government can engage current and potential data users in the analysis and application of big data around dementia, only a few of which are highlighted in this report. In this way, government can act as a catalyst through funding and other programming to stimulate innovation around dementia care that may support innovation and improvement across a range of diseases.

Government can also support the more effective use of big data on dementia by ensuring that data are always treated in a secure way that respects confidentiality and does not lead to inappropriate use, such as genetic discrimination. Furthermore, governments can use research, and economic and accounting policy to ensure that data are appropriately valued, widely shared, and used to its fullest extent across the health and social systems, regardless of whether they are public or privately organised and run on a non-profit or for-profit basis. Governments can also use international agreements to support further the sharing and use of data across countries grappling with the challenge of dementia and stimulate action in those that have not yet developed plans. Fundamentally, however, all of these steps require governments to acknowledge the importance of big data in shaping and supporting the fight against dementia and the importance of using a combination of mechanisms such as funding, regulation, and advocacy. None of these vehicles for change will be sufficient on their own.

Table 2.2. Promising areas of innovation in response to governmental role in cure, care and regulation

Promising areas of innovation	Selected examples from OECD countries and/or resources
	Measures of gait and walking speed: Motoric Cognitive Risk (MCR) syndrome, is identified by the combination of slow walking pace (<1m/s) and cognitive complaints (Verghese et al., 2012) Blood tests (Burnham et al., 2013) Retinal scans and Gaze trackers (Australia) (Frost et al., 2014) Genetics testing (i.e. 23andme) (United States) (Roberts et al., 2013) Neuroimaging (differentiation between subtypes) (Thompson et al., 2007) Phone monitoring (Petersen et al., 2014) Social engagement/conversation (Dodge et al., 2014)
Treatments and new drug categories	Brain stimulation (Ash et al., 2014) Tauopathies (TauRx clinical trials; Diamond et al., 2013) Proteomics (i.e. α-sheet peptides) (Hopping et al., 2014)
Models of care	Interlinks (European Union) Dementia Village (Hogeway) Netherlands Dementia Friendly Cities (Canada) PACE (United States)
Economic supports to caregivers	Tax credits, labour support policy (Bill 21, Ontario) Caregiver Benefit Program (Nova Scotia, Canada) Cash and Counselling (United States) (Carlson et al., 2007) Long-term care insurance (Germany) (Keefe, 2011)
Data harmonisation and techniques for data sharing	BioSHARE (European Union) BioBRICK (United States) DataSHIELD Method (Doiron et al., 2013) DataSHaPER approach (Fortier et al., 2011) BioBrick™ Public Agreement (BPA)
Clinical trials	Clinicaltrials.gov (United States and Worldwide) Support for advancing clinical trials. Shortage of volunteers to participate in clinical trials and studies (Scott et al., 2013).
Regulation	Genetic information non-discrimination Act (2008) (United States) Preamble to the Additional Protocol to the Convention on Human Rights and Biomedicine (European Union) Disability Discrimination Act 1992 (Australia) – Genetic information can be used by insurers to restrict access to certain life insurance policies. Belgium, Norway, Austria, Denmark, France, Lithuania, Portugal, Sweden, and Germany have all introduced or passed legislation to prohibit genetic discrimination.

Note: This table was generated by conducting an environmental scan of the recent literature produced by Alzheimer and dementia specific charitable and governmental websites, from worldwide policy statements (i.e. OECD, WHO) and from Conference proceedings, of the Alzheimer Association's International and Alzheimer Disease International from years 2012 to 2014.

Notes

1. This chapter has been written by Natalie Warrick, MSc, Dalla Lana School of Public Health, Institute of Health Policy, Management and Evaluation, University of Toronto, Canada; Adalsteinn Brown, PhD, Institute of Health Policy, Management and Evaluation, University of Toronto, Canada; and Kirk Nylen, PhD, Ontario Brain Institute, Toronto, Canada.

2. Whereas acute care is the largest sector in terms of costs in most health care systems, long-term care is the largest sector contributor to dementia costs in Canada (ASC, 2009; CIHI, 2011). The Canadian experience is illustrative of the challenges in improving dementia care. By 2038 the proportion of Canadians 65 years and older living with dementia receiving community care will increase to 42.7% compared to 19.5% with severe dementia in 2008 (NPHSNC, 2013; CIHI, 2010).

References

23andme, "About Us", Retrieved from www.23andme.com/.

Alzheimer's Australia (2014), "Statistics". Retrieved on June 24, 2014 from www.fightdementia.org.au/understanding-dementia/statistics.aspx

ADI – Alzheimer Disease International (2014a), "Government Alzheimer Plans", Alzheimer's Disease International, London, Retrieved from www.alz.co.uk/alzheimer-plans.

ADI (2014b), "Helping Carers to Care Intervention", Alzheimer's Disease International, London, Retrieved from www.alz.co.uk/helping-carers-to-care.

Alzheimer Society of Canada. (2009). Rising Tide: The Impact of Dementia on Canadian Society. Toronto: ASC, 2009.

Auyoung, S., B. Howell, A. Randhawa, N. Warrick, J. Yi, P. Rabinow and A. Stavrianakis (2007), *Synthetic Biology & Intellectual Property*, OpenWetWare.

Ash, E., N. Bregman, O. Moore, K. Amos and A. Zangen (2014), "Transcranial Magnetic Stimulation of Deep Brain Regions in Alzheimer's Disease", Alzheimer's Association International Conference, Copenhagen.

Bancej, C.M., R. Garner, P. Fines, D. Manuel, A.J. Zycki, R. Wall, T. Nguyen and J. Bernier on behalf of the NPHSNC Working Group on the Health and Economic Modelling of Neurological Conditions (NPHSNC) (2013), "Report on the In-Person Stakeholder Consultation".

Barnes, D.E. and K. Yaffe (2011), "The Projected Effect of Risk Factor Reduction on Alzheimer's Disease Prevalence", *The Lancet Neurology,* Vol. 10, No. 9, pp. 819-828.

BioBricks Foundation (2014), "BioBricks Programs", Retrieved on May 31, 2014 from http://biobricks.org.

Burnham, S.C., N.G. Fau, W. Wilson, S.M. Laws, D. Ames, J. Bedo, A.I. Bush, J.D. Doecke, K.A. Ellis, R. Head, G. Jones, H. Kiiveri, R.N. Martins, A. Rembach, C.C. Rowe, O. Salvado, S.L. Macaulay, C.L. Masters and V.L. Villemagne (2013), "Alzheimer's Disease Neuroimaging Initiative. Australian Imaging, Biomarkers and Lifestyle Study Research Group. A blood-based predictor for neocortical Aβ burden in Alzheimer's disease: results from the AIBL study", *Molecular Psychiatry*, pp. 1-8.

Cameron, P., G.R. Pond, R.Y. Xu, P.M. Ellis and J.R. Goffin (2013), "A Comparison of Patient Knowledge of Clinical Trials and Trialist Priorities", *Current Oncology*, Vol. 20, No. 3, p. e193.

CIHI – Canadian Institute for Health Information (2011), "Health Care Cost Drivers: The Facts", Ottawa, Retrieved from https://secure.cihi.ca/free_products/health_care_cost_drivers_the_facts_en.pdf

CIHI (2010), "Supporting Informal Caregivers – The Heart of Home Care", *Analysis in Brief: Health System Performance*, Retrieved from https://secure.cihi.ca/free_products/Caregiver_Distress_AIB_2010_EN.pdf.

Canadian Institute of Health Research, http://www.cihr-irsc.gc.ca/e/46475.html.

Canada Parliament, House of Commons, Standing Committee on Environment and Sustainable Development (2014), "Minutes of Proceedings", Meeting No. 72. June 16, 2014, 36th Parliament, 1st Session (Online), available at www.parl.gc.ca/LEGISInfo/BillDetails.aspx?Language=E&Mode=1&billId=6257110 (July 30, 2014).

Carlson, B.L., L. Foster, S.B. Dale and R. Brown (2007), "Effects of Cash and Counseling on Personal Care and Well-Being", *Health Services Research*, Vol. 42(1p2), pp. 467-487.

Doiron, D., V. Ferretti, P. Burton, Y. Marcon, A. Gaye, B.H.R. Wolffenbuttel and I. Fortier (2013), "Data Harmonization and Federated Analysis of Population-based Studies: The BioSHaRE Project", *Emerging Themes Epidemiology*, Vol. 10, No. 12.

Dodge, H.H., M. Bowman, J. Zhau, N. Matteck, K. Wild and J. Kaye (2014), "A 6-Week Randomized Controlled Trial to Increase Social Interactions Using Home-based Technologies Improved Language-Based Executive Function", Alzheimer's Association International Conference. Copenhagen.

Department of Health, Social Services and Public Safety (2011), "Improving Dementia Services in Northern Ireland: A Regional Strategy".

Diamond, M. (2013). "Tau As a Prion: Mechanisms and Implications", *Alzheimer's & Dementia: The Journal of the Alzheimer's Association*, Vol. 9, No. 4, pp. P673-P673.

Fortier, I., D. Doiron, J. Little, V. Ferretti, F. L'Heureux, R.P. Stolk and P.R. Burton (2011), "Is Rigorous Retrospective Harmonization Possible? Application of the DataSHaPER Approach Across 53 Large Studies", *International Journal of Epidemiology*, Vol. 40, No. 5, pp. 1314-1328.

Frost S, et al. (2014), "Retinal Amyloid Fluorescence Imaging Predicts Cerebral Amyloid Burden and Alzheimer's Disease", *AAIC Abstract O3-13-01,* Alzheimer's Association International Conference, Copenhagen.

Fujisawa, R. and F. Colombo (2009), "The Long-Term Care Workforce: Overview and Strategies to Adapt Supply to a Growing Demand", *OECD Health Working Papers*, No. 44, OECD Publishing, Paris, http://dx.doi.org/10.1787/225350638472.

Hopping, G., J. Kellock, R.P. Barnwal, P. Law, J. Bryers, G. Varani and V. Daggett (2014), "Designed α-sheet Peptides Inhibit Amyloid Formation by Targeting Toxic Oligomers", *eLife*, Vol. 3, e01681.

Jacobs, A. (2009), "The Pathologies of Big Data", *Communications of the ACM*, Vol. 52, No. 8, pp. 36-44.

Keefe, J.M. (2011), "Supporting Caregivers and Caregiving in an Aging Canada", *IRPP Study No. 23*, Montreal: Institute for Research on Public Policy.

Lin, J.S., E. O'Connor, R.C. Rossom, L.A. Perdue and E. Eckstrom (2013), "Screening for Cognitive Impairment in Older Adults: A Systematic Review for the US Preventive Services Task Force", *Annals of internal medicine*, Vol. 159, No. 9, pp. 601-612.

Lee, L., M.J. Kasperski and W.W. Weston (2011), "Building Capacity for Dementia Care Training Program to Develop Primary Care Memory Clinics", *Canadian Family Physician*, Vol. 57, No. 7, pp. e249-e252, Retrived on June 28, 2014 from www.uwo.ca/fammed/csfm/siiren/primaryhealth/rounds_documents/Oct_11_2012_Linda%20Lee%20Oct%2011%202012%20Enhancing%20Dementia%20Care_JAGS_2010.pdf.

National Institutes of Health (2012), "Genetic Information Nondiscrimination Act (GINA) of 2008", Retrieved on June 26, 2014 from www.genome.gov/24519851.

Norton, S., F.E. Matthews, D.E. Barnes, K. Yaffe and C. Brayne (2014), "Potential for Primary Prevention of Alzheimer's Disease: An Analysis of Population-based Data", *The Lancet Neurology*, Vol. 13, No. 8, pp. 788-794.

Ontario Legislative Assembly (2014), "Employment Standards Amendment Act (Leaves to Help Families)... ", Bill 21, 40th Parliament, 2nd Session, Toronto: The Assembly (assented to Apr. 29, 2014).

OECD (2014), "Unleashing the Power of Big Data for Alzheimer's Disease and Dementia Research: Main Points of the OECD Expert Consultation on Unlocking Global Collaboration to Accelerate Innovation for Alzheimer's Disease and Dementia", *OECD Digital Economy Papers*, No. 233, OECD Publishing, Paris, http://dx.doi.org/10.1787/5jz73kvmvbwb-en.

OECD (2013), "Data Driven Health Care Innovation, Management, and Policy", OECD, Paris, http://www.oecd.org/sti/inno/data-driven-innovation-interim-synthesis.pdf.

OECD (2011), Help Wanted? Providing and Paying for Long-term Care, OECD Publishing, Paris, http://dx.doi.org/10.1787/9789264097759-en.

Parmar, R., I. Mackenzie, D. Cohn and D. Gann (2014), "The New Patterns of Innovation", *Harvard Business Review*, January-February, pp. 86-95.

Prince, M., M. Guerchet and M. Prina (2013), "Alzheimer's Disease International: Policy Brief for Heads Of Government: The Global Impact of Dementia 2013-2050", Alzheimer's Disease International, London.

Petersen, J., D. Austin, J. Yeargers and J. Kaye (2014), "Unobtrusive Phone Monitoring as a Novel Measure of Cognitive Function", *AAIC Abstract P1-184*, Alzheimer's Association International Conference, Copenhagen.

Roberts, J.S. and J. Ostergren (2013), "Direct-to-Consumer Genetic Testing and Personal Genomics Services: A Review of Recent Empirical Studies", *Current Genetic Medicine Reports*, Vol. 1, No. 3, pp. 182-200.

Scott, T.J., A.C. O'Connor, A.N. Link and T.J. Beaulieu (2014), "Economic Analysis of Opportunities to Accelerate Alzheimer's Disease Research and Development", *Annals of the New York Academy of Sciences*, Vol. 1313, No. 1, pp. 17-34.

Stabile, M., A. Laporte and P.C. Coyte (2006), "Household Responses to Public Home Care Programs", *Journal of Health Economics*, Vol. 25, No. 4, pp. 674-701.

Suzuki, R., D. Goebert, I. Ahmed and B. Lu (2014), "Folk and Biological Perceptions of Dementia Among Asian Ethnic Minorities in Hawaii", *American Journal of Geriatric Psychiatry*.

TauRx Therapeutics (2014), "Information About TauRx", Retrieved on May 31, 2014 from http://taurx.com/.

Thompson, P.M. and L.G. Apostolova (2007), "Computational Anatomical Methods as Applied to Ageing and Dementia", *British Journal of Radiology*, Vol. 80, pp. S78-91.

TimeBanks USA (2014), *About Us*, June, Retrieved from http://timebanks.org/about/.

U.S. Department of Health and Human Services (2014), "National Plan to Address Alzheimer's Disease", Retrieved from on June 29, 2014 from http://aspe.hhs.gov/daltcp/napa/NatlPlan.shtml.

Verghese, J., C. Wang, R.B. Lipton and R. Holtzer (2012), "Motoric Cognitive Risk Syndrome and the Risk of Dementia", *Journals of Gerontology Series A: Biological Sciences and Medical Sciences*, gls191.

Wimo, A. and M.J. Prince (2010), *World Alzheimer Report 2010: The Global Economic Impact of Dementia*, Alzheimer's Disease International.

Chapter 3

Big data approaches to dementia: Opportunities and challenges

Geoffrey Anderson, Robin Buckle, Giorgio Favrin, Stephen Friend, Daniel Geschwind, Howard Hu, Stephen Oliver, Ronald Petersen, Martin Rossor, Peter St George-Hyslop and Bin Zhang[1]

Although diverse neurodegenerative diseases cause dementia, they share two important features. First they have long pre-clinical periods with varying disease progression trajectories. Second, their causation is driven by both genetic and environmental factors. Big data approaches will provide opportunities to better understand disease progression and the complex interplay between genes and the environment. Although there are many important biological, clinical and population data sets available, there are key data limitations. Overcoming these limitations and reaping the benefits of linked data will require successful resolution of several challenges including: making existing and newly acquired data available in open access platforms that protect participant privacy; harmonising data so that they can be usefully merged; improving our collection of population-based exposure data; curating databases; and managing expectations. Appropriate funding needs to be set aside for all phases of a big data discovery paradigm as part of a balanced portfolio of research.

3.1. Introduction

Dementia is a diagnostic term encompassing a diverse set of diseases that are characterised by a progressive debilitating failure of cognitive function after a pre-existing period of normal cognitive activity. The majority of these diseases are disorders of advanced age. The common diseases include Alzheimer's disease (AD), vascular cognitive impairment, fronto-temporal dementia (FTD), and dementia with Lewy bodies (DLB). However, there are numerous other causes, not all of which are degenerative and some of which are treatable. Although the neurodegenerative dementias differ in their clinical and neuropathological presentations, they share at least two important characteristics.

The first unifying feature amongst these diseases is that many of them appear to have long (5-10 years) preclinical periods in which the disease is active but not readily clinically detectable. During these preclinical stages, the disease may be manifest only by very subtle changes that may be detected by biochemical, imaging, or behavioural studies. These changes, when considered individually, are insufficient for a definitive diagnosis. It has been suggested that multimodal methods that combine genetic risk profiles with subtle changes in cognitive biochemical, immunological and neuroimaging biomarkers might be useful in detection of individuals in the early stages of these diseases. Such multimodal profiles could also be used early in the disease to predict progression and/or future therapeutic response. An attempt to address this concept through a big data approach is exemplified in a recent DREAM challenge (www.synapse.org/#1synapse:syn2290704).

The second and perhaps most obvious shared characteristic is that most of these diseases have complex patterns of transmission in which both genetic and environmental factors play important roles. Thus, in each of these diseases, there are familial cases in which the condition appears to arise predominantly from a single genetic defect. However, in many of the neurodegenerative diseases, a significant proportion of cases likely reflect the interaction between multiple genetic and environmental factors. The individual effect size of each of these genetic and environmental factors is probably low. As a result, identifying these factors, teasing apart their individual contributions, and understanding the hierarchy of their interactions continues to be a major challenge. To meet this challenge, we need to understand the disease as a system in which synergistic or antagonistic interactions between factors are likely to be more important than those factors' own individual contributions.

This chapter assesses the potential benefits of big data approaches that mine both deep biological datasets (e.g. containing genetic, epigenetic, imaging, biomarker and other biochemical/molecular data) and broader population-based datasets (e.g. data on exposure to external risk factors, data from medical records, care homes, geospatial modelling and, potentially, even commercial datasets). We show here that this multifaceted big data approach could help uncover: 1) new information on fundamental biological processes (e.g. gene: environment interactions; 2) potential biomarkers of early disease (e.g. combinations of genetic and environmental factors); and 3) previously unsuspected modalities that modify disease progression and/or symptoms (e.g. lifestyle changes, effectiveness of drugs approved for other indications). This review also highlights some of the hurdles that will need to be overcome both in terms of data quality and correlating data from different sources.

3.2. Anticipated outcomes and benefits of big data approaches

The reason why big data approaches may now be timely arises from a collision of both positive and negative drivers.

The negative driver is principally the observation that, so far, as with other complex diseases, no single method has provided the necessary answers. The existing tools have necessarily focused on "sweet spots" where they are most effective. The big data approach complements these other approaches by providing a different point of view on information that has not been explored to date.

The positive driver is that this approach allows the integration and statistical correlation of information across different size scales (from subcellular to whole population) and information types (from biomedical to exposomics).

The use of large sets of data culled from sources such as hospital and clinical practice medical records, care homes, diagnostic laboratories, and pharmacies; as well as non-medical data such as commercial credit card and mobile phone usage and performance on Internet-based cognitive games provide the possibility to test a wide range of interactions on a scale that is not practical by existing hypothesis-driven approaches. These wide-ranging interaction analyses have the possibility of throwing up unanticipated interactions such as the discovery of the unintended benefits from therapies prescribed for other diseases. An example of the latter is the discovery of the effect of metformin prescribed for diabetes mellitus to lower cancer risk. Such discoveries could have a number of utilities. It is possible that such interactions could themselves be immediately used preventatively or therapeutically. Conversely, the discovery could be used as a probe to direct further experiments to dissect the underlying biological signalling and metabolic pathways involved. This might then uncover novel molecular targets that are therapeutically tractable.

Big data approaches using population-based information allow the inclusion of anonymised and pseudonymised medical records attached to biological data. It also allows the incorporation of data on exposure to a variety of environmental risk factors (using external and internal markers) in order to see how they interact with biological risk factors such as genetic variants. There are already data to suggest that some environmental risk factors, such as socio-economic status or early childhood education, modulate risk for dementia. Naturally, systems or network biology becomes an ideal framework to integrate clinical, medical, biological data and environmental data in dementia because it systematically explores the interaction or causality relationships among a large number of variables in an unbiased manner. A pioneer study in this direction was the identification of co-expressed gene networks in AD using only gene expression data (Miller et al., 2008; 2010). A subsequent study tried to integrate large scale genetic, gene expression and clinical data in late-onset AD using a multi-scale network framework (Wild, 2012). These approaches need be extended to incorporate many other types of clinical, medical, biological and environmental data such as imaging, epigenomic and proteomic information.

As with all experiments investigating correlations between multiple noisy variables, the analyses tend to become more robust when the investigated datasets are larger, and to become more susceptible to error when small datasets are investigated. This therefore encourages the notion that, using properly curated data, national and international collaborative big data approaches are more likely to yield the new information that is needed to complement the existing, typically hypothesis-driven, biological approaches.

The sponsorship of such large-scale international collaborative efforts would be a clear mandate for OECD and G7 Summit legacies to facilitate these types of international big data collaborations.

3.3. Gene-environment interaction: Genomics and exposomics

Given that a key characteristic of dementia is that in the vast majority of cases it is the result of some complex interaction between the gene and environmental exposure, a key objective is to link and analyse data that brings together what we know about the gene with what we know about exposure. Exposomics is a new approach to exposure assessment that recognises the challenge and promise of gathering accurate current and historical data on individual human exposures. As defined by Wild, "the exposome is composed of every exposure to which an individual is subjected from conception to death…it requires consideration of both the nature of those exposures and their changes over time" (Wild, 2012). Wild defines three broad categories of non-genetic exposures: internal (e.g. metabolism, endogenous circulating hormones, body morphology, physical activity, gut microflora, inflammation, lipid peroxidation, oxidative stress, ageing), specific external (e.g. radiation, infectious agents, chemical contaminants, environmental pollutants, diet, lifestyle factors, occupation, and medical interventions) and general external (e.g. social capital, education, financial status, psychological and mental stress, urban–rural environment and climate (Wild, 2012). Although both genomics and exposomics are independently powerful tools for understanding disease, combining these methods has the potential to open new avenues for discovery and innovation.

3.4. Information types and information sources for big data experiments

The strength of big data approaches lies in the ability to simultaneously acquire biological, clinical/medical and population-based data and use this information to investigate the interaction of factors within these data realms in order to understand: 1) they coalesce to modulate risk for disease and modify disease expression; 2) how combinations of these data elements might be used to diagnose the disease in its early stages and monitor its prevalence within populations; and 3) how targeting these biological/social/environmental processes might be exploited to both prevent and treat dementia.

Biological data

The biological data elements typically addressed include: 1) RNA and protein expression profiles in healthy and diseased tissue at single cell, regional or whole-organ levels; 2) genetic information about healthy and disease-affected individuals, typically in the form of genome wide single nucleotide polymorphism (SNP) data and/or whole-exome sequence data (WES) or whole-genome sequence data (WGS); and 3) epigenetic data on site-specific DNA modifications and histone acetylation. This information may be acquired from cellular models including induced pluripotent stem cells (iPS cells), as well as from invertebrate and vertebrate animal models. It can also be obtained from human tissues in which case it is often linked to pseudononymised clinical data on diagnostic status, cognitive function, biochemical/serological/neuroimaging and/or neuropathological information. Presently, this type of complex biological and clinical data has been collected for a modest numbers of cases and controls (10-5000). Examples of such databases include the Alzheimer's Disease Neuroimaging Initiative (ADNI), Alzheimer's Disease Genetics Consortium (ADGC), GEO-PD, as well as various public repositories of cell type and regional RNA and protein expression data such as the Allen Brain Institute.

Clinical/medical data

Clinical data typically contain information about symptoms; diagnostic tests including blood, CSF and brain-imaging tests; rates of disease progression; types of treatment given for the disease of interest or for other diseases; the impact of that treatment; the presence of other illnesses and comorbid factors; and some information about the physical, social and economic environment. This information can be linked, in pseudonymised databases, to specific biological data as above. It is expected that, within the next 1-5 years, these types of complex multimodal data will be acquired for larger numbers of cases and controls (10 000-500 000). Examples of these larger datasets include the UK dementia platform, UK 1000 Genomes Project, DZNE Rhineland dementia project and the Mayo Clinic Study of Aging. Many of these cohorts contain not only cross-sectional data, but also longitudinal data. Additional potential sources of such detailed biological and clinical information are commercial databases arising from trials of new medicines and candidate diagnostics.

Population-based data

Broad population-based information can also be acquired on much larger numbers of individuals from medical records, long-term care records and other population-based epidemiological studies. Although these datasets are usually not coupled with deep biological characterisation, important data can be gleaned from medical records, records from long-term care institutions about diagnosis, hospitalisations, drug exposure, socio-economic status, exposure to various environmental risks such as diet, smoking, occupation, lifestyle factors such as cognitive engagement, or exercise. Some of these items (e.g. early childhood education and ongoing cognitive engagement) are already thought to impact risk and/or progression of disease. It is expected that, over the next decade, the information content of population-based datasets will dramatically increase through the acquisition of low-cost DNA sequencing which allows the inclusion of both genomics-wide sequence and transcription profiling data on large numbers of individuals. Other potential sources of data include various types of commercial data such as data on credit card, mobile phone, Internet, or social media usage. These commercial data likely contain information about lifestyle (e.g. diet, alcohol and cigarette consumption, exercise, etc.). In addition, changes over time in the complexity of some parameters such as social engagement and shopping habits can reflect changes in cognitive activity that might describe the early stages of disease. We should also anticipate a more engaged public where both healthy individuals and individuals who are sick will track their own phenotypic data. There are devices today that allow exercise and sleep, heart rate and blood pressure, to be captured that represent emerging mechanisms to engage the public as full partners in developing models of disease. Such information is likely to be generated by smart phones and wearable devices in three ways: 1) passively-tracking activities such as exercise using the accelerometers, 2) structured tests where someone is directly asked to do a test for characteristics such as cognitive decline, and 3) surveys and questions that people can answer in real-time multiple times each day.

3.5. Limitations and challenges

Despite the recent heightened interest in big data approaches, and their clear potential for providing insights into complex diseases, there are important data challenges. One is the uneven distribution of information content. For instance, molecular, genomic and neuroimaging datasets usually have large amounts of intensely detailed quantitative information that has typically been acquired only on relatively small, often specialised, subject cohorts. In many instances, these subjects have been collected for specific reasons (e.g. the characterisation of genetically defined cohorts of subjects with particular disease-causing genetic variants, or datasets of highly homogeneous affected subjects at specific stages of the disease assembled for clinical trials). As a result, these disease-specific datasets may not be particularly representative of the overall disease of interest. Conversely, large population cohorts, that might more accurately reflect the type of cases encountered in the community, usually have very little molecular or genetic data. Currently very few datasets have proteomic and metabolomics data on large numbers of subjects even though proteome and metabolomics data are likely to be a very rich source of difference information between individuals. Another limitation is the variable nature of data collected across cohorts. This "variability" arises from several factors; these include differences in the precise measurement tools applied, and differences in the quality or reliability of data even when the same or similar measurement tools are used. They also include differences in ethnicity, behaviour, and, if unmeasured, differences in nutritional and environmental exposures. A major confound is simply data that are not collected in some cohorts (i.e. missing data).

There are several challenges to successfully addressing these limitations.

The first challenge will be to ensure that existing and newly acquired data are made available in open access platforms in ways that protect the anonymity of research participants. As described below, there are already examples in which reanalysis of publicly available data have provided important new insights into disease mechanisms. Data that are accessible only to a limited number of investigators clearly represent a potential bottleneck in the discovery pathway. One example of potentially highly useful information that is known to exist, but is not widely available, is the large amounts of normative data obtained from the very well-characterised control cohorts within the numerous clinical trials being undertaken on neurodegenerative diseases. An important mandate of OECD and G7 would be to implement methods by which these anonymised data could be made available more widely.

A second important challenge that must be resolved by consortia involved in big data projects on dementia will be to harmonise at least some of the data tools and/or to develop methods that allow highly similar datasets to be merged. This will be simpler for some data items (e.g. imputing genotypes from different forms of genetic information such as single nucleotide polymorphisms in genome-wide association studies, whole-exome sequencing, and whole-genome sequencing studies). Conversely it may be impossible to merge data for cognitive and behavioural measures if the tests that were used examined very different functions (e.g. episodic memory versus executive function). This challenge is already being faced by longitudinal clinical and population-based studies, where new follow-up data are often collected with tools or instruments that are either more sensitive (e.g. 1.5T MRI versus 7T MRI), or not available (e.g. positron emission tomography-based ligands for Aβ, tau, etc.) during the earlier data collections.

A third challenge is the continued lack of accurate exposure assessment tools that are available for application in very large populations. Geospatial-based exposure assessment tools (such as imputation of individual exposures to air pollution using regional air pollution monitoring data) have been useful in gaining some insights but remain relatively imprecise. Measurements of internalised pollutants in blood, urine, and other media are useful for estimation of on-going exposure, but have very limited utility as a measure of cumulative or historical exposures.

A fourth critical challenge is based upon the realisation that a key foundation for success in big data experiments will be the use of carefully curated databases, appropriate replication cohorts, development of effective systems biology approaches to integrate multiple types of data from different sources into biologically plausible models for dementia, and thoughtful use of validating biological experiments that may involve a range of carefully chosen model organisms. Appropriate funding needs to be set aside for all phases of this big data discovery paradigm.

A fifth, and not insignificant, challenge will be to manage expectations. As with any newly emerging field, the excitement of the new field often results in an overstatement of what the new method is realistically likely to achieve in practical terms. Big data approaches will unquestionably bring new insights into the cause, biology, and diagnosis of disease. The understanding arising from these insights may help plan experiments to develop and test new therapies and preventative strategies. However, as with any other experimental tool, big data experiments are unlikely to be the panacea for all the problems that afflict research into dementia. A balanced portfolio of approaches is likely to be more successful than an overemphasis of any single tool.

3.6. Examples of national approaches

The potential for the application of big data approaches in dementia to: provide insights into the basic biology, clinical diagnosis and risk prediction; identify specific patient subgroups with unique and important disease course profiles (rapid deterioraters, positive therapeutic responders); monitor disease burden in the population and thereby manage health care resource allocations has attracted notice in many countries with national health care programmes. These include health care programmes in, alphabetically, Canada, Europe, Japan, Korea and the United Kingdom. In these countries, the national health care programmes contain a wealth of longitudinal health data on the population from cradle to grave. For instance, the National Health System (NHS) in the United Kingdom contains information on a population of 63 million.

In many countries, this has already led to several initiatives to investigate ways in which electronic medical health records can be accessed for the purpose of research. For instance, the United Kingdom has established initiatives such as the Clinical Practice Research Data Link, and the Farr Institute of Health Informatics Research to develop the skills and infrastructure to link electronic health records with educational, housing, pollution, accident and demographic datasets, and ensure interoperability with the UK and EU data sharing initiatives. There are also strategic partnerships being built such as the ELIXIR initiative that will integrate life science data repositories (e.g. those set up by the European bioinformatics Institute (EBI) including ENA, UniProt, PDBe, ArrayExpress archives, as well as informatics tools such as ENFIN, IMPACT, and SLING. In the United Kingdom, but also elsewhere, such database and data analysis initiatives have been complemented by investment in large-scale whole genome sequencing of population cohorts (e.g. the 100 000 Genome Project announced by the UK Department of Health). In parallel, for the longer term, there are prospective, long-term, large-scale programmes such as the UK Biobank Initiative that will prospectively collect biological samples and data on lifestyle, genetics and health for 500 000 participants, aged 40-69 years. 100 000 participants are being recruited into a dementia focused prospective cohort which includes 3T brain MRI and 1.5T body MRI together with cognitive testing and bio-sampling. Finally there is a UK Dementias Platform which correlates a number of existing clinical and population cohorts, including

UK Biobank, that represent approximately 2 million participants in ongoing studies that will be linked in a single informatics hub and can be mined for information on a variety of biomarkers and biological data. Such large-scale initiatives in both data collection, data analysis, and data sharing on platforms that are interoperable by investigators worldwide represent a key element in making the vision of big data approaches to dementia realistic. As mentioned earlier, one recent foray into the use of multiple datatypes from multiple different cohorts applied to solve a clinically relevant problem in dementia is the recent DREAM challenge (www.synapse.org/#1synapse:syn2290704).

Note

1. This chapter has been written by: Geoffrey Anderson, PhD, Institute of Health Policy, Management And Evaluation, University of Toronto, Canada; Robin Buckle, MD, Medical Research Council, London; Giorgio Favrin, PhD, Cambridge Systems Biology Centre & Department of Biochemistry, University of Cambridge, United Kingdom; Stephen Friend, MD, PhD, Sage Bionetworks, Seattle, United States; Daniel Geschwind, MD, PhD, Neurogenetics Program, Department of Neurology, Center for Autism Research and Treatment, Semel Institute, David Geffen School of Medicine, University of California, Los Angeles; Howard Hu, MD, Dalla Lana School of Public Health, University of Toronto, Canada; Stephen Oliver, Cambridge Systems Biology Centre & Department of Biochemistry, University of Cambridge, United Kingdom; Ronald Petersen, MD, PhD, Department of Neurology, Mayo Clinic and Foundation, Rochester, United States; Mayo Clinic Alzheimer's Disease Research Center, Mayo Clinic and Foundation, Rochester, United States and Division of Epidemiology, Department of Health Sciences Research, Mayo Clinic and Foundation, Rochester, United States; Martin Rossor, MD, Dementia Research Centre, UCL Institute of Neurology, University College London, United Kingdom; Peter St George-Hyslop, MD, Tanz Centre for Research in Neurodegenerative Diseases, University of Toronto, Canada and Cambridge Institute of Medical Research, Addenbrookes Hospital, Cambridge, United Kingdom; Bin Zhang, PhD, Department of Genetics and Genomic Sciences, Icahn School of Medicine at Mount Sinai, New York.

References

Miller, J.A., M.C. Oldham and D.H. Geschwind (2008), "A Systems Level Analysis of Transcriptional Changes in Alzheimer's Disease and Normal Aging", *Journal Neuroscience,* Vol. 28, pp. 1410-1420.

Miller, J.A., S. Horvath and D.H. Geschwind (2010), "Divergence of Human and Mouse Brain Transcriptome Highlights Alzheimer Disease Pathways", *Proceedings of the National Academy of Sciences of the United States,* Vol. 107, pp. 12698-12703.

Wild, C. (2012), "The Exposome: From Concept to Utility", *International Journal of Epidemiology*, Vol. 41, pp. 24–32, PubMed PMID: 15277625.

Zhang, B. et al. (2013), "Integrated Systems Approach Identifies Genetic Nodes and Networks in Late-Onset Alzheimer's Disease", *Cell*, Vol. 153, pp. 707-720.

Chapter 4

Opportunities for businesses, foundations and stakeholders

John J. Alam[1]

There is a shared interest in the discovery and advancement of novel therapeutic interventions for dementia and in particular, in interventions that address disease progression. The history of drug development suggests that the approach to discovery can be either biochemically target-based or phenotypic. There are opportunities and challenges for dementia in both of these approaches. The creation of an accessible big data resource for dementia could provide a "base camp" to support a range of efforts including opportunities around disease categorisation, therapies for vascular dementia, disease modifying drugs, symptomatic therapies, and preventive and risk-modifying strategies. Bringing broad and deep data together can provide opportunities to provide a better understanding of disease categories and progression that will allow for more focused efforts around cardiovascular medicines and symptomatic treatments. Inclusion of data on exposures and risk factors will allow for preventive therapies and non-pharmaceutical approaches to risk factor modification. Better accounting of the full range costs of dementia will clarify the rate of return on new interventions and spur investment in research and discovery.

4.1. Introduction

This chapter examines the opportunities for businesses, foundations and stakeholders to link detailed biologic and clinical data with population-based data. As the major common interest for these diverse constituencies is the discovery and advancement of novel therapeutic interventions, the focus will be on the opportunities around this topic, particularly, on the advancement of novel medicines that address dementia disease progression. This chapter describes some of the challenges in treatment and prevention discovery in dementia both in terms of biology and economics. It provides some lessons and insights from drug discovery in other diseases and ends with the identification of some key opportunities for linking biological/clinical data with population-based data.

4.2. The dementia therapeutics discovery problem

As is widely known, there are no disease-modifying drugs available for any of the dementias. In the best case scenario, for Alzheimer's disease (AD), the first disease-modifying agents may become available later this decade, though this is by no means certain. Also, if such drugs were successful in clinical studies, they would likely be only representative of the first step towards the US 2025 goal of "preventing or curing" AD. For vascular dementia and other dementias aside from Alzheimer's, such prospects are much lower. From a drug discovery standpoint, dementia research represents an especially daunting challenge, which explains this dearth of therapeutic prospects.

At a high level, the strategy to discovering novel drugs can be divided into two main approaches: target-based and phenotypic (Swinney and Anthony, 2011). Target-based drug discovery is an approach that aims to discover and develop molecules that specifically inhibit proteins and/or biochemical pathways that have been otherwise identified to be important for disease activity and/or progression. In contrast, phenotypic drug discovery is an approach that aims to discover and develop molecules that lead to a particular pharmacologic or physiologic effect at either a cell biology or whole animal (or human) level; e.g. blood pressure lowering or blocking of inflammation. For neither R&D approach is dementia well suited.

Target-based approaches have worked best in infectious disease (e.g. anti-virals that target viral proteins that are critical for replication of specific viruses) and oncology (e.g. kinase inhibitors that inhibit pathways activated by mutations in oncogenes that drive disease progression in specific, well-defined cancers). Target-based drug discovery has also been successful in certain chronic disease contexts, such as cardiovascular medicine (CV). The difference between dementia research and CV research is that with CV research, the field solved single problems that targeted specific mechanisms one at a time over 50+ years, while the dementia field is trying to simultaneously solve multiple components of the overall drug discovery problem in ten years to achieve the 2025 goal of curing or preventing dementia.

Phenotypic approaches can only be applied, and have been successful, when there are clear pharmacologic/physiologic endpoints (i.e. a "phenotype") that can be readily measured pre-clinically and is translatable clinically. With regard to dementia, the challenge has been that the only relevant and measurable pharmacologic/physiologic effect has been improvement of cognition, an effect that is difficult to ascertain pre-clinically and/or translate pre-clinical results into clinical results. Cognition as an endpoint measure in dementia research has been successful with symptomatic therapies. However, only mixed target-based and phenotypic approaches have been successful in generating new medicines. For disease modifying agents, the use of slowing cognitive decline as a measure, has proven to be too unreliable and cumbersome from a time and expense standpoint to evaluate and validate effects of specific molecules (or mechanisms) that would come out of the phenotypic approach to drug discovery.

4.3. The "BHAG – Big Hairy Audacious Goal" for big data in dementia research

For the business context, Collins and Porras (1996) have coined the term "Big Hairy Audacious Goal" to focus organisations on a single long-term goal that they define as "...an audacious 10-to-30-year goal to progress towards an envisioned future." For big data in dementia research, the potential BHAG is the full integration of all data, information and knowledge around the biology of dementia. This is a clear major opportunity for therapeutic development and involves assisting the R&D ecosystem (public, private; academic, non-academic) to take on what sometimes appears to be the insurmountable challenges around drug discovery and development for biological complex conditions such as dementia; especially when the amount of data and information around this biology is growing exponentially. Starting with Alexander Fleming and the discovery of penicillin, the paradigm around breakthroughs in drug discovery have been about "connecting the dots" around otherwise seemingly unconnected biological observations, often as a result of serendipity. The opportunities for such serendipitous connections of people and science are increasingly difficult to realise because the whole endeavour around dementia is organisationally large and dispersed, and the amount of data is simply too great for any individual scientist or even groups of scientists to incorporate all available information. All of this is then exacerbated by the general inability to ascertain easily the quality of publicly available data and information. The opportunity and perhaps promise of "big data" for pharmaceutical R&D then is to connect the scientific dots in a systematic and rigorous manner, thereby removing the serendipity aspect of drug discovery. The Human Brain Project (Kandel et al., 2013), based in Europe, is perhaps the best example of an effort to achieve this type of systematic integration of data and knowledge to the understanding of human disease; and at the same time illustrates the challenges of comprehensively solving the problem. However, beyond the organisational challenges, there are major issues around access to data, data transfer (bandwidth and time required to transfer the amount of data that are being considered) and computational power that will need to be solved, none of which are necessarily solvable in the time frames that are being considered. The more nuanced challenge may be around the nature of the analysis and whether existing computational approaches can mimic at a large scale what individual scientists and drug discovery accomplish in terms of problem solving and pattern recognition when they do connect the dots. That is, whether the artificial intelligence capabilities are sufficiently developed to go beyond integrating data to solve the underlying biologic problems that will need to be solved in order to advance dementia therapies. And so, while accomplishing this full integration of all data/information/knowledge is the BHAG for big data, it is unlikely to be realised in the near term.

4.4. "Base camp" for big data in dementia research

Because the BHAG is meant to be very long-term (decades long) and inherently not obviously realizable today, Collins (2005) has also proposed the concept of "base camp". He develops the concept by drawing on an analogy to climbing Mt. Everest, where climbing to the summit is the BHAG. In that context, ascending the summit is not considered a single activity because taken as one step is too daunting a task; instead it is viewed as a two-step process: first, the establishment of a base camp, which then allows for the second step ascent to the summit. Although the base camp requires more resources and time than the subsequent ascent, it is more realizable and a more predictable outcome with the appropriate investment of people and time. In dementia research, the "base camp" and the opportunities around therapeutics development for all concerned stakeholders to linking biologic and clinical data to population-based data are related to the benefits of what otherwise has been referred to as "stratified medicine" (Trusheim et al., 2007). While stratified medicine and personalised medicine are often used interchangeably, for this chapter the term "stratified medicine" will be utilised to emphasize the objective to identify groups (populations) of patients who share certain biologic and clinical characteristics that allow for optimal discovery and development of medicines; while personalised medicine at an extreme is about optimising care at an individual patient level. The fundamental challenge for pharmaceutical R&D for chronic disease is biologic complexity and heterogeneity, and as a result, generally the industry has not been successful in developing disease-modifying drugs for complex chronic disease. Dementia is of course no exception. Where the industry has been successful is in infectious disease, genetic disorders, and then subsets of major diseases where the biology is more straightforward and understood (e.g. specific cancer subtypes which have identified driver cancer mutations). The objective of stratified medicine then is to simplify the biologic problem to benefit across the entire R&D value creation cycle. For discovery, specific mechanisms (targets) that are important to drive disease in specific patient segments or subsets can be identified. For early clinical development, the heterogeneity size of clinical studies would be substantially reduced, and larger treatment effects would allow for earlier identification of therapeutically active agents. For late stage development, the benefit-risk ratio would be improved which would allow for a more predictable path to approval and commercialisation. Beyond R&D, stakeholders and payers would receive more benefits for any given level of use of new medicines.

4.5. Specific opportunities

Disease categorisation

When it comes to dementia, the most immediate need around stratified medicine, and perhaps most addressable with available data is simply better categorisation of dementia, and better understanding of categories and sub-categories of the disease. Until recently, the lack of access to tissue has set apart brain disease from nearly all other diseases in which understanding of specific tissue pathology and often even profiles of blood tests have allowed for categorisation of many, if not most diseases (a major exception may be pulmonary disease, where access to tissue pre-mortem is also a challenge). With dementia and other brain disorders, there is no easy access to pre-mortem biopsy material; and cerebrospinal fluid is at best an indirect measure of what is occurring in the brain, as it is compartmentalised from brain interstitial fluid in a way the peripheral blood compartment is not from most well-perfused peripheral organs. The clear opportunity today is to utilise neuroimaging (MRI, functional MR, PET) and electrophysiology (EEG, MEG) to characterise patient subsets, but to this point, we have only scratched the surface of this opportunity. Effectively, we are where cancer research and cancer genetics were a few years back when there were isolated case series and studies that evaluated DNA mutation and genetics of small numbers of tumors. Today, there are multiple studies emerging, where the DNA of large numbers of patients with various tumors is being systematically sequenced and whole new approaches to characterising tumor type and patient categorisation for cancer is rapidly emerging. Moreover, the systems are being developed to link the tumor genetics data with clinical data at a population basis in order to create true linkage of biologic/clinical data with population-based data. Eventually, the expectation is that within the next few years, we will be creating a new way to stratify tumors, and with it creating new ways to practice cancer medicine.

In the field of dementia, to begin to be able to achieve what has been accomplished in cancer medicine, neuroimaging in particular must be applied systematically and more broadly than we do today, then the data must be captured in a format where it can be broadly disseminated in an open format to link it to population-based data. Towards that objective, efforts are underway to develop algorithms that can be applied to neuroimaging data (e.g. atrophy) at a population level. An additional challenge is that the population-based data needs to be strengthened in terms of specific cognitive and functional outcomes. A clear advantage in cancer research is that the outcomes (survival, tumour response by imaging, disease recurrence, etc.) are objective, and certainly survival is well captured at the population level (perhaps the other endpoints are also reasonably well captured). Hard endpoints, such as survival and institutionalisation in dementia occur late in the disease course, and even for an endpoint such as mortality, often it is not linked to dementia as the cause and is instead ascribed to an inter-recurrent acute event, such as infection. For much of the disease course, the impact of dementia on patients and care partners is simply not captured in standard population-based databases such as health care utilisation databases. To be able to develop population-based data for standardised measures of cognition or function must be developed and implemented for either simple patient or care partner reported outcome (or perhaps health care provider assessed). Alternatively, algorithms must be developed that can utilise certain data to develop surrogates for those outcomes. One example of such an outcome assessment is the patient/caretaker based symptom inventory approach, developed by Rockwood et al. (2013), who used to identify in defined clinical cohorts within the broader Alzheimer's population, a broad categorisation where a slight majority of patients have "on symptoms", with aggressivity and increased activity being the major issues, while a large minority have "off symptoms", with decreased activity, apathy, and depression being the dominant symptoms. It would be of interest to know and understand whether this categorisation, or other such categorisation, hold up at broad population levels and tie them into other clinical, biologic, and health care utilisation measures.

Therapeutics for vascular dementia

A specific need, and with it an opportunity, lies in deep characterisation and development of diagnostic criteria and staging of vascular dementia (Series and Estri, 2012). If successful, it might lead to a specific opportunity for the pharmaceutical industry, as the success in cardiovascular medicine and the availability of therapeutics in that arena make it likely that the industry already has mechanisms and potentially active drugs available for vascular dementia. However, lack of consensus on diagnostic criteria, patient heterogeneity, and lack of hard outcomes measures make it a very challenging context to develop new drugs. The US FDA (United States Food and Drug Administration) has not approved any drugs for vascular dementia, and the two drugs for which an NDA (New Drug Application) was submitted, a major issue was whether vascular dementia comprised of a specific and definable enough indication for drug approval. Another issue is whether such indication would provide clinicians with sufficient guidance as to whom they should prescribe the medication. For business, aside from developing novel chemical entities for vascular dementia, if specific patient populations with definable disease course and outcomes could be identified, additional opportunities likely exist for repurposing existing cardiovascular medicines for either treatment or risk factor modification (see below also).

Disease modifying drugs for AD

The field is most advanced in terms of disease characterisation in Alzheimer's disease, where within the past several years the use of cerebrospinal fluid (CSF) and neuroimaging biomarkers has led to a better and more specific diagnosis with an understanding of the full spectrum of the disease from pre-symptomatic stage, to prodromal phase, to the development of frank, symptomatic Alzheimer's disease. This understanding that the disease is present many years in advance of what was previously thought of as the onset of the disease (i.e. onset of symptoms and/or frank dementia) should allow for earlier intervention with therapeutics that target the early stages of disease ("right drug, right stage of disease") (Sperling et al., 2005).

Multiple sclerosis (MS) presents an example of how moving to the earlier stages of the disease to better understand its stages and progression can open the way for successful therapeutics development. As is the case with AD today, at the end of the 1980s, the prospects for effective therapies for multiple sclerosis appeared bleak. Animal model data and clinical studies argued that an overactive immune system and subsequent inflammation played a major role in driving the disease. However, a series of clinical trial failures with the best available immunosuppressants (e.g. cyclosporine, azothioprine, cyclophosphamide, etc.) argued that the autoimmunity/inflammation hypothesis was wrong and the field needed to go back to defining the cause of MS and develop completely novel mechanistic approaches. Instead, by 1993, the first immunomodulatory therapy, interferon beta, demonstrated efficacy in MS and was marketed, followed by a series of therapies across a wide range of mechanisms but always with the immune system as the target (e.g. galantamer acetate, mitoxantrone, natalizumab, fingolimod, teriflunomide, etc.).

In retrospect, a major cause of failure with the initial wave of clinical studies in multiple sclerosis that targeted the immune system was that the studies were conducted in patients with advanced disease (i.e. chronic progressive MS). The field subsequently came to understand inflammation plays a very little role in disease activity and progression of these patients. Today, the scientific community would say that there is very little inflammation and the immune system has almost no role in patients with progressive MS; instead, disease progression in chronic progressive MS appears to be driven by a neurodegenerative process that requires novel treatment approaches directed at neural, rather than immune, mechanisms. The major innovation that led to the subsequent treatment successes was moving the intervention point earlier in the disease, to the relapsing phase when inflammation is abundant and is a major contributor to disease activity and progression.

Two factors allowed this move to earlier stages of disease in multiple sclerosis. The first is the data from large population-based longitudinal studies (such as Western Ontario, Mayo, and others) that defined the natural history of relapsing-remitting MS and demonstrated that a sizable portion, perhaps majority of such patients over 10-15 years develop progressive disease with substantial disability. Added to the clinical results was the availability of imaging (MRI and CT) that both allowed for earlier diagnosis and more importantly demonstrated that even patients with rare relapses and resolution often signify ongoing disease activity within the brain. The imaging data combined with the clinical data then provided the reasoning to apply what were otherwise pharmacologically potent agents to patient groups that were previously thought to be in too early stage of the disease to warrant such therapies. In addition, imaging provided the ability to diagnose patients at earlier stages of disease.

It is hoped that what has been achieved in multiple sclerosis can be replicated in the field of dementia. A major challenge will be that we do not have the time to conduct the longitudinal studies that were conducted in multiple sclerosis but, perhaps therein lies the opportunity with big data of being able to link together various ongoing natural history studies and broader population-based data to understand the long-term course of the disease in categories of patient populations (i.e. in a stratified manner).

Though understanding the spectrum of the Alzheimer's disease process is a major step forward, more needs to be done to understand subsets of patients with established Alzheimer's disease. Even in the lay public, it is well understood that different patients present different symptoms and signs (i.e. phenotypes); and scientifically it is clear that there is a broad range of genotypic risk factors, any one of which only impacts a minority of patients with Alzheimer's. Because of this clinical and biological heterogeneity, an emerging consensus is that within the broad population with established Alzheimer's dementia there are multiple disease types (Murray et al., 2011; Lam et al., 2013). Yet, to this point, new drugs are developed with an implicit assumption of homogenous disease processes and homogenous response as most studies include patients with "mild to moderate AD" (i.e. very broadly defined) and then assessed with more or less the same set of assessment tools despite often very different mechanisms of action. Moreover, in a number of recent clinical trials, while overall results did not indicate treatment effects, treatment effects were evident in specific subsets. While these results could be spurious, it may also indicate that some number of these therapies were effective in specific populations for which the mechanism was appropriate. However, the overall observed effects were diluted in broad, heterogeneous patient populations where the mechanism of the drug had little to no effect. Having a better understanding of which biologic mechanisms are relevant for which subsets of patients could substantially increase the probability of success for novel medicines in the established Alzheimer's disease population. In addition, gaining a better understanding of which clinical outcome measures had the most relevance for patient subsets would also increase probability of seeing positive treatment effects. At a minimum, such understandings would substantially reduce the cost of development because treatment effects would be more evident in substantially smaller studies.

One major limitation in dementia research for understanding populations that no disease modifying agents are currently available, as an inherent disease categorisation, is response vs. non-response to treatment. With one or more disease modifying agents with different modes of action and an understanding of who does or does not respond to different mechanisms, one can confirm disease mechanisms. As well, analysing which categories of patients respond to different therapies provides insights on which biologic mechanisms are most important in different categories of patients, thereby providing opportunities to optimise outcomes in specific populations of patients, and perhaps at an individual patient basis. Efforts to understand multiple sclerosis at this level through analysis of all available clinical, biologic, and population-based data are underway. One example is Orion Bionetworks (www.orionbionetworks.org), a non-profit public-private partnership that is "dedicated to accelerating the discovery of next-generation diagnostics, treatments and cures of brain disorders by harnessing the power of high-performance computing and data analytics to discover and develop predictive models from integrated biomarkers, biosensor and phenotypic data." The learnings from these efforts are likely to inform on opportunities and how best to progress with big data initiatives for dementia; and as such, studying these activities is an opportunity for dementia researchers, particularly after the first disease modifying agents are available.

Symptomatic therapies

In the meantime, symptomatic therapies are available for AD and linking biologic/clinical data to population-based data is a potential opportunity for patients by providing a better understanding of how to best use the available therapies. A recent randomised clinical trial showed that despite disease progression, patient outcomes are better when they stay on cholinesterase inhibitor therapy rather than discontinuing therapy (Howard et al., 2012). However, in the real world, the great majority of patients discontinue therapy because the benefit to an individual patient is simply not evident as there is no way to ascertain in their specific context whether or not they are doing better than they would have if they had discontinued treatment, although they are doing worse than when they started treatment. It is also very likely that while there is a population-level benefit to continuing treatment, for many individual patients there is likely not any benefit and only a subset are truly benefiting. Having a predictive model that would say which specific subsets of patients should continue on available therapies would reinforce the decision to continue therapy for both clinicians and patients/care partners. On the other side, the patients who would be identified to not benefit from continuing could then be encouraged to enroll in clinical trials of novel symptomatic therapies. More broadly, having a better understanding as to who does or does not respond to currently available therapies would potentially accelerate development of novel therapies, both symptomatic and disease modifying, by providing means to handle the variability that is inherently introduced with heterogeneous clinical response to current therapies.

Preventive therapies and risk factor modification

Beyond therapeutic interventions, understanding better patient stratification and disease categories in dementia are likely to provide major opportunities around preventive therapies. A number of risk factors for development of dementia have been identified, but the impact of any one risk factor tends to be modest when dementia is viewed as a whole (Patterson et al., 2008, Purnell et al., 2009; Norton et al., 2014). The modest associations are not surprising given heterogeneity of criteria for diagnosis and underlying disease pathology. In recent phase 3 trials, as much as thirty percent of ApoE4 non-carrier "Alzheimer's" patients likely did not have Alzheimer's, as they did not have evidence of amyloid plaque in their brain by PET scanning (Fitzgerald, 2014); given that results in a rigorously defined clinical trial that was run at top academic medical centers, a higher proportion of Alzheimer's "cases" in epidemiologic studies are likely to not have Alzheimer's pathology. The problem of diagnosis is of course compounded for vascular dementia and mixed dementia. Moreover, recent genetic data indicates after stratification (e.g. male vs. female, or ApoE4 carrier vs. non-carrier) the genetic risk factors are different, making it likely that risk factors otherwise are likely to be different between different population strata. For these reasons, it is likely that re-assessing risk factors at the population level after more rigorous application of clinical and biologic data to establish specific diagnoses and phenotypic/genotypic stratification is likely to lead to a fundamentally different understanding of risk factors for dementia by specific population sub-categories than we have today.

If more specific higher-odds ratio biologic risk factors were to be identified, there would be an opportunity for the development of dementia prevention therapies of branded medicines similar to those that are marketed today for other indications. Potential opportunities include anti-diabetic agents (e.g. GLP-1 agonists), anti-inflammatory agents for Alzheimer's disease, anti-platelet agents for vascular dementia, or cholesterol-lowering agents for either indication. Many of these have been tried as therapeutic agents for established dementia, often with mixed results; but they are generally considered to have the potential to have a greater impact in the prevention context, particularly in the secondary prevention context – after symptom onset and before dementia onset. However, the industry is reluctant to assess these agents in that context because of general concerns around prevention therapies: low clinical event rates resulting in long clinical studies, unrecognised medical need, reimbursement issues, etc. Indeed, the pharmaceutical R&D model as a whole is not well suited for developing prevention therapies. Many of these issues would be addressed with the identification of population subsets of patients with both a higher risk of developing dementia and identified specific dominant but modifiable biologic mechanism(s) that drive that risk. Identification of such population subsets and biologic drivers could also potentially open new business opportunities for modifying risk and prevention around diagnostics and monitoring, as well potentially novel non-pharmaceutical interventions such as integrated solutions that could include nutrition, exercise, computer gaming, social media, etc. (Han and Han, 2014).

Economic case for investing in dementia research

Finally, for both the near and long term, a somewhat separate, high-level opportunity is to frame the economic arguments for why we must develop new drugs for dementia. The macroeconomic arguments have been made; i.e. there is a major societal cost to dementia. However, as opposed to other major public health problems such as HIV, through much of the course of pre-dementia and dementia the costs are not direct medical costs, rather a broader burden to society – caretaker burden, institutionalisation costs, as well as hidden economic costs, including both patient and caretaker productivity. In contrast with HIV, the medical care system costs were obvious, particularly to governments and policy makers, and the economic benefits of novel therapies came back to the governments and insurance companies that paid for the new therapies. In the case of dementia, in the short term, much of the economic benefits will not come back to those who pay for novel treatments (Hurd et al., 2013). As a result, particularly for therapies targeting early phases of the disease process (e.g. early mild cognitive impairment), there is a potential commercialisation risk that payers will be reluctant to pay for such treatments when the economic benefit is either to someone else or is so many years down the line. A better understanding of how costs carry through different stages of disease and subsets of patients could provide incentives to the industry to develop clinical development programmes and target patient populations that would provide the greatest health economic benefits (as well as providing the greatest health benefits as discussed in the rest of the paper). In addition, as privacy concerns around sharing population-based data is one of the obstacles to advancing big data initiatives, a better understanding of the macroeconomic benefits to society would be a balancing offset to the societal concerns regarding privacy, i.e. the societal level benefit-risk equation around privacy is improved by making the benefit more tangible (in addition, of course to minimising the privacy risks).

4.6. Opportunities

In summary, linking detailed biologic and clinical data to population-based data provides a number of near-term and long-term opportunities towards accelerating medicine development for dementia. The major potential near-term opportunities identified in this paper are as follows:

- The development of a deeper and better understanding of the broad disease categories and patient population subsets for the major dementias that should decrease the time, risk, and costs of drug development of dementia therapies.
- Specific understanding of diagnostic criteria and patient subsets for vascular dementia that potentially would allow the evaluation of established CV medicines as disease modifying drugs for the indication.
- Specific understanding of patient subsets for patients with established Alzheimer's dementia, potentially optimising the use of approved symptomatic therapies, as well accelerating the discovery and development of disease modifying agents for the indication.
- Specific and better understanding of risk factors for development of dementia, potentially accelerating the development of preventive therapies. Understanding of risk factors for dementia might also create new business opportunities for non-pharmaceutical-based approaches to risk factor modification.
- Better understanding of the health economic impact of dementias by disease category and patient sub-type, which would provide additional incentives to public and private sectors to invest in dementia research; as well as to overcome hurdles to advancing big data and other initiatives to accelerate new therapeutics discovery and development.

Note

1. This chapter has been written by John J. Alam, MD, EIP Pharma, LLC, Cambridge, United States.

References

Collins, J. (2005), *Good to Great and the Social Sectors*, Harper Collins, New York.

Collins, J. and J. Porras (1996), "Building Your Company's Vision", *Harvard Business Review*, Vol. 75, pp. 65-77.

Howard, R., R. McShane, J. Lindesay et al. (2012), "Donepezil and Memantine for Moderate-to-Severe Alzheimer's Disease", *New England Journal of Medicine*, Vol. 366, pp. 893-890.

Kandel, E.R., H. Markram, P.M. Matthews et al. (2013), "Neuroscience Thinks Big (and Collaboratively)", *Nature Reviews Neuroscience*, Vol. 14, pp. 659-664.

Lam, B., M. Masellis, M. Freedman, D.T. Stuss and S.E. Black (2013), "Clinical, Imaging and Pathological Heterogeneity of the Alzheimer's Disease Syndrome", *Alzheimer's Research & Therapy*, Vol. 5:1

Murray, M.E., N.R. Graff-Radford, O.A. Ross et al. (2011), "Neuropathologically Defined Subtypes of Alzheimer's Disease with Distinct Clinical Characteristics: A Retrospective Study", *The Lancet Neurology*, Vol. 10, pp. 785-796.

Patterson, C., J.W. Feightner, A. Garcia et al. (2008), "Diagnosis and Treatment of Dementia: Risk Assessment and Primary Prevention of Alzheimer's Disease", *Canadian Medical Association Journal*, Vol. 178, pp. 548-556.

Purnell, C., S. Gao, C.M. Callahan and H.C. Hendrie (2009), "Cardiovascular Risk Factors and Incident Alzheimer Disease: A Systematic Review of the Literature", *Alzheimer Disease and Associated Disorders*, Vol. 23, pp. 1-10.

Rockwood, K., M. Richard, C. Leibman, L. Mucha and A. Mitniski (2013), "Staging Dementia from Symptom Profiles on a Care Partner Website", *Journal of Medical Internet Research*, Vol. 15, e145

Seriesn H. and M. Estri (2012), "Vascular Dementia: A Pragmatic Review", *Advances in Psychiatric Treatment*, Vol. 18, pp. 372-380.

Sperling, R.A., C.R. Jack and P.S. Aisen (2011), "Testing the Right Target and Right Drug at the Right Stage", *Science Transnational Medicine*, Vol. 3, No. 111, p. cm33.

Swinney, D.C. and J. Anthony (2011), "How Were New Medicines Discovered?", *Nature Reviews Drug Discovery*, Vol. 10, pp. 507-519.

Trusheim, M.R., E.R. Bendt and F.L. Douglas (2007), "Stratified Medicine: Strategic and Economic Implications of Combining Drugs and Clinical Biomarkers", *Nature Reviews Drug Discovery,* Vol. 6, pp. 287-293.

Chapter 5

How we can work together on research and health big data: Strategies to ensure value and success

Donald T. Stuss, Shiva Amiri, Martin Rossor, Richard Johnson, Zaven Khachaturian[1]

Creating a big data resource that brings different data sources together so that they can be shared internationally is challenging. This effort needs to be guided by principles that ensure the integrity, excellence and multi-disciplinarity of the science, while at the same time recognising the importance of privacy and data security. The chapter provides examples and lessons from several existing efforts. It suggests that putting the patient at the centre and developing partnerships are essential and recognises the value of learning from each other about governance and data standardisation policies. It concludes that we need to have open dialogue among existing big data initiatives, that we develop a shared commitment to privacy by design, and that we need to embark on specific efforts to test the feasibility and sustainability of international data sharing.

5.1. Introduction

The "why" for a big data approach to dementia is covered in other papers presented at this workshop and is driven by the enormous social, health and economic impact of neurodegenerative diseases. The focus of this paper is on the "how" – what has to be done to achieve success in sharing data at different levels, including cross-political boundaries. This paper is guided by the important work of other groups in particular the 2013 OECD consultation *Unlocking Global Collaboration to Accelerate Innovation for Alzheimer's Disease and Dementia* (OECD, 2014). This consultation brought together experts from member countries to help identify the key factors related to the "how" and this paper works from three specific issues that were defined in that consultation:

- key barriers to data deposition, access, exchange and linkage, and areas for international co-operation,
- policies and good practices that foster and enhance the performance of research for Alzheimer's from the existing large datasets and that can serve as the standards for new ones,
- the value and economic impacts to the global AD community – including the international scientific community, patients, clinicians and companies – of a tiered networking structure to facilitate the co-ordination of large data sets at national, regional and international levels.

Organisations from many countries have started to wrestle with these issues including International Alzheimer's Disease Research Portfolio in the United States, Ontario Brain Institute (OBI) in Canada, Alzheimer's Disease Neuroimaging Initiative (ADNI), and the European (Joint Programme Neurodegenerative Disease Research) JPND programme. This paper draws on the OBI as the source of specific examples but the principles are drawn from the experience of all the authors. The paper is divided into six sections. The first describes the importance of a vision of science organisation which provides a framework for the "how". This is followed by foundational principles for maximising the value of data. The third section considers the value of the approach to reinforce the need to share data. The last three sections emphasize practical utility: pragmatic steps needed to ensure success; risks and obstacles to success, and potential mechanisms to mitigate the risk; and recommendations on next steps.

5.2. Organisation of science

The scientific process has always included the public disclosure of new knowledge gained from research, and the methods of acquiring such knowledge. What has changed over time, however, is the complexity of the scientific challenges required to answer urgent questions. This complexity often demands massive and diverse data, a demand with significant costs and obstacles. That is, data are not only the domain of the individual researcher, but a resource that can and should be shared. Sharing can be of many types. One can think of sharing as a group with a common purpose sharing a resource, for example, a group sharing a car to drive from Ottawa to Toronto. Sharing can be much broader than that. For example, governments and private partners can work together to create a highway infrastructure that will support different vehicles going to different places. This latter type of sharing is where we are focused – shared infrastructure/research resources. Sharing of this kind provides the possibility of the same data being used by multiple users for multiple ends.

Gathering and sharing data is now possible because data are increasingly collected in digital form, storage is less of an issue with decreasing costs and availability, and there is a growing need to organise long-term storage to have critical impact. This is reflected in international approaches and the growing number of initiatives to consolidate data being collected locally, nationally, and internationally. An example that has led the way in big data sharing practices is the Alzheimer's Disease Neuroimaging Initiative (ADNI) which began in 2005. ADNI allows for the sharing of neuroimages from across the globe in defined projects. Also gaining momentum is crowdsourcing the analytics of big data which has led to the Alzheimer's Big Data Challenge, developed by Sage Networks and the Global CEO Initiative on Alzheimer's Disease (CEOi) and announced at the White House in 2013. In this initiative, Alzheimer's datasets were made available to scientists all over the world to identify new biomarkers and advance diagnostic innovation through the use of open source data.

One of the arguments of this paper is that research systems (researchers, industry, end users of evidence, patients) need to work together to ensure that research value is optimised. In this way, the use and quality of data is also optimised. One example of large-scale research system integration is the Ontario Brain Institute, funded by the Province of Ontario to ensure that science has both long-term and short-term impact (Stuss, in press). The selection of questions to be answered, and mental health and neurological disorders to be tackled, was based first on the excellence of the science and, in addition, on the importance for the province, both health and economy. That is, the province wanted science with impact. This vision of science has consequences for the organisation of research. It requires integration of all components of the research cycle across the province: patients, advocacy groups, industry, government, clinicians and researchers. It needs individual scientific and clinical excellence. It also requires integration and sharing of data, a collaborative approach resulting in increased sample sizes to answer research questions with greater significance. Impact through data requires multiple practical steps: development of an informatics platform to allow aggregation and sharing of data; ensuring that the informatics platform is as equivalent in standards as possible to existing neuroscience platforms (e.g., ADNI); long-term secure storage and methods of encryption and de-identification to allow sharing; ensuring quality of data standardisation by having clinicians and scientists agree on common assessments and training; and developing commonalities of tools and assessments both within and between disorders studied.

This approach also increasingly extends beyond the basic research enterprise to translational research and clinical trial designs. For example, the recently announced public-private Global Alzheimer's Platform (GAP) in the United States is motivated by the realisation of the need for new R&D infrastructure built around big data that extends into clinical trials. This new platform is being designed to increase the speed and flexibility of AD clinical trials by creating a standing network of fast-start sites, large-scale longitudinal datasets, and well-characterised patient cohorts identified through new data science that can be integrated with a continuing adaptive clinical trial framework. At the heart of GAP is a comprehensive data management system and data sharing mechanisms enabling faster patient selection for individual clinical trials and novel big data components for natural history studies.

It also encompasses non-traditional approaches such as the use of consumer big data. In one corporate example, Optum Labs in the United States – working with the Mayo Clinic and a broad consortium of university-based academic medical centers – has developed a "Natural History of Disease" discovery tool for AD and dementia using over

150 million claims-based, de-identified records to promote advanced data exploration. This enables the personalisation of the patient experience, and to explore health services and markers in the "at risk" interval prior to diagnosis to AD and dementia.

5.3. Principles of development

The excellence of the science is foundational. This covers all aspects of the scientific enterprise: the methods used (e.g., which genetic approaches, which imaging measures); the questions asked (e.g., will the science resulting from using the data make real breakthroughs); and the quality, experience and productivity of researchers (i.e., all the effort and expense in setting up the infrastructure has to have a real potential of success). The recognition of the multidisciplinary nature of the research is essential in the context of dementia. It is becoming increasingly evident that, even though we characterise a disease by a single name (e.g., Alzheimer's disease), this label is used to cover many complex neurodegenerative diseases (Khachaturian, 2012). The mechanisms underlying "a" disease are multiple even at the genetic level, and the expression of the disease from genes to behaviour can be affected by multiple variables, including diet, early developmental factors such as maternal/paternal care, the factors that enhance cognitive reserve that might offset the onset of a disease such as exercise, education, bilingualism, music, and environmental factors (Ontario Brain Institute, 2013; Craik et al., 2010; Stern, 2012; Rosen et al., 2011; Barnes et al., 2009). Together, these may result in building "cognitive reserve" (Stern, 2012). These facts directly imply that multidisciplinary assessments are necessary if we wish to find valid bio- (and other) markers to characterise subgroups of patients, and to have the most sensitive outcome measures. The lack of consideration of the heterogeneity of the disease symptomatology and underlying mechanisms may well be the reason for the lack of success in clinical trials (Callaway, 2012). This approach has been taken by the EU Joint Programme – Neurodegeneration Research (JPND) which funds research across all neurodegenerative disorders recognising the commonalities of disease processes, exemplified by the phenotypic expression of *C9orf 72* mutation disease (JPND Research News, 2013).

The fact that neuroscience is no longer a single field is emphasized by the United States National Academies. "Recognizing that neuroscience is not, of course, really a single field is important. Rather, it is a multidisciplinary enterprise including diverse fields of biology, psychology, neurology, chemistry, mathematics, physics, engineering, computer science and more. If scientists within neuroscience and related disciplines could unite around a small set of goals, the opportunity for advancing our understanding of brain and mental function would be huge" (Institute of Medicine, 2008).

The blurring of the lines of distinction between diseases has implications for how science is organised. OBI has developed a matrix approach (Figure 5.1). This is a major reason for standardisation of evaluations and data gathering within disease groups, and as much as is feasible across diseases. This allows finer characterisation of potential subgroups within diseases, an important step in clinical trials. Analyses across diseases maximise understanding of the impact of co-morbidities, and create the potential to address the mechanisms of the diseases (e.g., what is the role of inflammatory processes across different disease cohorts?).

Figure 5.1. OBI's Matrix Approach for data analysis across diseases and across data modalities

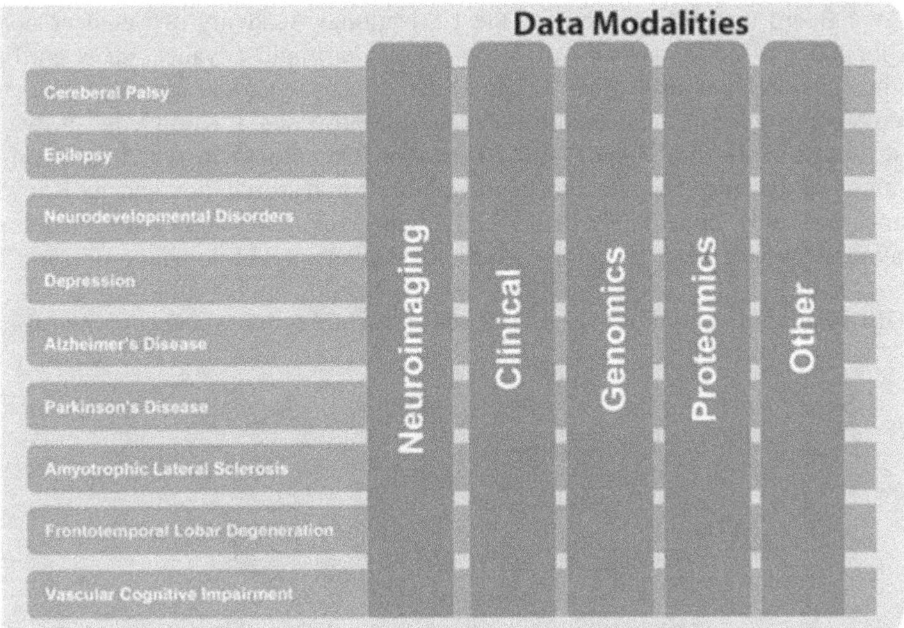

The quality of the data is an essential principle: garbage in, garbage out. This means harmonisation of data gathering and storage. To the degree possible, data structure should follow international standards to allow federation of data. Harmonisation includes not only acceptance of a standard approach, it also demands constant training and quality monitoring.

The data are often in the form of personal health information derived from individuals where privacy protection and data security are paramount. Data security and privacy are foundational principles in the construction of informatics platforms. This means working with the Privacy Commissioners from the very beginning; Privacy by Design (Cavoukian and Reed, 2013; Cavoukian et al., 2014) has also been recognised internationally by the US Federal Trade Commission and in October 2010, regulators from around the world gathered at the annual assembly of International Data Protection and Privacy Commissioners in Jerusalem, Israel, and unanimously passed a landmark Resolution recognising Privacy by Design as an essential component of fundamental privacy protection (Data Protection and Privacy Commissioners, 2010).

Finally, there has to be a clear definition of the different taxonomies of data, since not all data are created equal. There is frequent mention of the 3Vs: **V**olume; **V**ariety (see above on heterogeneity); and **V**elocity. Taxonomies may also be considered as types of data; e.g., personal health information, de-identified data. How one deals with the different taxonomies for different questions needs to be considered in the development of the informatics platform, in particular the security measures related to data sharing. In this regard, the OBI's informatics platform, Brain-CODE, has instituted three different zones depending on the type of data, who might have access, and under what circumstances (Figure 5.2).

Different taxonomies of data also need to be linked to the growing recognition of the need for new taxonomies of disease, including AD and dementia. In an influential report,

Toward Precision Medicine: Building a Knowledge Network for Biomedical Research and a New Taxonomy of Disease (National Research Council of the National Academies, 2011), the Board on Life Sciences of the US National Academy of Sciences not only called for modernised taxonomies of disease based on rapid advances in scientific and biomedical research but also for new approaches to integrating research data with clinical data, environmental data, and health outcomes. It proposed a Knowledge Network of Disease infrastructure based on: "an 'Information Commons' in which data on large populations of patients become broadly available for research use and a 'Knowledge Network' that adds value to these data by highlighting their inter-connectedness and integrating them with the evolving knowledge of fundamental biological processes."

Figure 5.2. OBI's informatics platform has a three zone structure for data collection, storage and release

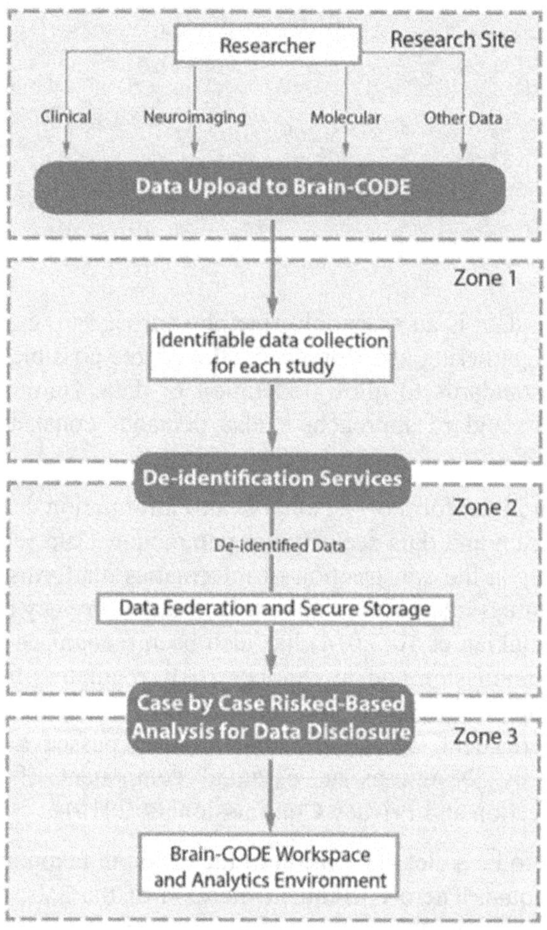

Success of a big data approach to science requires partnership. Patients and advocacy groups have to believe in the value of the approach and be involved in all aspects of the endeavour; to not only volunteer and consent for research in a way that allows sharing of data, but to push government, researchers and clinicians to move toward a new vision of research because it benefits the patients. The important role of clinicians as the front-line contact with patients and the acceptance of the effort demanded of clinicians to do the standardised assessments and data input must be acknowledged (Wilhelm et al., 2014).

Basic science researchers must accept the importance of working in an integrated system, which maximises the sharing of knowledge, and also the transfer of basic knowledge into products and improved health systems. Government(s) must be willing to change regulatory processes and funding modalities to encourage the integrated approach. Industry has to consider early, pre-competitive sharing, not only as a means to its own survival, but also as a tool to advance science more quickly. And finally, there is an essential role for social philanthropy.

Perhaps the most important principle is open and transparent communication amongst all partners.

5.4. New value proposition: Moving from silos to systems

The value lies in the creation of a system, integrating all partners from the very beginning of research to catalyse, facilitate, and maximise scientific, health care and policy, and commercialisation efforts. The standardisation of assessments and the sharing of data have many positive outcomes. Assessment standardisation in all of the clinical centres involved in the research means consistency of clinical evaluation at the research level across regional and national boundaries and an increase in the number of individuals involved in research activities. The sample size increase has obvious benefits for research power, and the study of mechanisms of disorders across diseases.

With a greater number of individuals involved, and careful standardised characterisation, the potential exists for good data and high quality clinical trial platforms. There is an increased opportunity to observe the variability and heterogeneity of disease expression (Georgiades et al., 2013; Stuss and Binns, 2008), and develop well-characterised sub-groups. A direct and completely linked corollary is improved diagnosis and treatment. This should be attractive to improve clinical trials and commercialisation of neuroscience research, in both neurotechnology and neurotherapeutics, i.e., the potential benefit of targeted pharmacological and behavioural treatments. In essence, there is a real opportunity for product development based on a "personalised medicine" approach. And this will only be enhanced if the full data sets from all past clinical trials are shared (Eichler et al., 2013).

Equally important is the need to link both research "deep data" and an individual's and population "broad data" (defined as the data in the health system – often the greatest breadth of data is in single payer arrangements – of the patient's medications, usage of the health system, changes in personal health over time, the existence of co-morbidities, and the associated cost of this usage) about AD and dementia with the vast amounts of data generated during clinical trials. It is important to take advantage of the new policies adopted by many biopharmaceutical companies, social philanthropists, and government funders to increasingly share clinical data. This provides a unique opportunity for health policy and health service delivery research. The OECD should identify and catalogue these new policies and trends across different regulatory jurisdictions. For example, the US National Academies recently released a new report proposing guiding principles for responsible sharing of clinical trial data (National Research Council, 2014).

As indicated in the 2014 OECD report on harnessing big data, "big data is, however, not just a quantitative change, it is a conceptual and methodological change" (OECD, 2014). The goal then, to truly maximise the value of big data, is to establish a system where basic science flourishes because of patient characterisation and removing boundaries around diseases are removed to facilitate studies of mechanisms of disorders;

where the informatics platform and data sharing within and across diseases provide an opportunity not only for hypothesis driven research, but for chance finding, data mining, and the creation of new hypotheses; where discovery and treatment are more closely linked; where industry works closely with researchers to implement their discoveries into new products; where the new products for improved patient health has an economic benefit through the creation of new companies and jobs; where the creativity of the researchers and the needs of individuals with disorders fuel new research questions and ideas; where the network of patient advocacy groups and health charities, as well as knowledge exchange with primary health care givers push early and rapid uptake of new diagnoses and new treatments; and where collaborative linkages and partnerships are created to harness the value of these approaches. There are technical challenges of bringing together datasets even within jurisdictions, let alone beyond national borders, and harmonising these linkages internationally is the biggest challenge (Khachaturian, 2013). But they are not insurmountable, and the outcomes appear to be well worth the effort (Cukier and Mayer-Shoenberger, 2013). There is a value to the international scientific community, with economic impacts of shared R&D resource/structure, to facilitate international collaborative research.

5.5. Practical suggestions to make it succeed

Identifying effective strategies that support the "how" is not an easy matter, especially in the context of continuing competitive approaches between scientists, institutions, universities, and even countries. There are several practical approaches we propose to facilitate success.

1. Putting the patient at the centre of activities guides the design of an appropriate system, including embedding patient privacy, confidentiality and security into our informatics platform. The OECD has emphasized the importance of greater harmonisation of privacy-respectful monitoring and research activities (OECD, 2013a).
2. The value of data is dependent on its quality and standardisation of data, including common data elements selected by those involved (e.g., researchers, clinicians, patients and advocacy groups), is crucial. To be internationally valuable, the standardisation should accept already developed international methods where they exist and where appropriate, and adopt an internationally collaborative approach to developing new common data elements.
3. Alignment of the development of the platform with the research vision and implementation is foundational, from the decision on which diseases to study, to what measurement modalities to develop and standardise, and to the value of the platform for analytic capacity.
4. Developing a partnership approach to big data that involves working with researchers and their institutions on legal, ethical, and privacy matters is critical, and open transparent communication is required.
5. The development of a governance framework with policies, security and privacy audits, interactions with research ethics boards and academic institutions is essential. The more universal this framework is, the easier the data linkages and sharing.

6. The architecture for integration and federation to link and leverage existing data sets, and to work with other groups both locally and internationally must be established. This has been exemplified in the neuroimaging research world, where a task force on neuroimaging data sharing was created with a goal of developing tools to eventually automate data sharing from raw to derived data (Poline et al., 2012).

5.6. Threats to success and methods of mitigation

The question most often asked is – why should researchers share data, since the reinforcement system rewards competition, not sharing: the successful grant awardee has in effect ensured that someone perhaps just a little way down the rank does not get funded. It is important to realise that there is no real conflict between sharing and individual success; the emphasis here is on the construction of a shared resource for additional data generation, use, and hypothesis generation. Important questions, such as the genetic basis of a specific disease, require data from many more patients than one researcher/clinician has. Ultimately, if the system is set up properly, there will be so much data that there is no need to be competitive – everyone can win.

Another threat is the notion that "big data" might change the fundamental and historical nature of science. The value of big data has been questioned. Is the gathering of big data and the development of data mining approaches in direct conflict with hypothesis driven basic research? Major discoveries that have changed medical science and have had significant health implications have resulted from individual scientists, or a small group of scientists, focusing on specific questions (e.g., the discovery of insulin; the cure for polio, small pox, HIV; the development of magnetic resonance imaging). But is this a false dichotomy? Establishing the matrix approach to data gathering with standardisation across diseases not only provides big data for "discovery" but also a structure that enables hypotheses of mechanisms of disease to be tested across diseases. It is our contention that a big data approach and hypothesis-driven basic research are not exclusive but mutually supportive. Answers from data mining can create new hypotheses to be tested. There is also significant value in observational studies, as well as very large longitudinal data bases on well characterised populations as they provide the opportunity to validate in prospective studies the prognostic value of various putative genetic and other biomarkers.

Moreover, the accumulation of big data is not a goal onto itself. Big data, however, has several positive advantages that argue for its value. First, trends and patterns can be observed in large data sets that lead to creation of new insights and hypotheses to be tested. The second is the growing social need for "personalised" or "precision" medicine, which requires understanding all the facets affecting individual health, including environmental, cultural, and psychosocial experiences. There is a need for improved specific diagnoses. Third, with the growing awareness of the heterogeneity of disease, treatment and clinical trials need to be specifically targeted to the appropriate subgroups. Since we do not know which characteristics are important to define subgroups, it is important to include the potential sources of heterogeneity (e.g., genetics, environmental influences, historical impacts, etc.) so that subgroups can be statistically extracted from larger pools of individuals.

Does a patient focus hamper basic science? An emphasis on output and translation may appear to be at the risk of basic discovery research. Some counter-arguments are presented above. But, in addition, there must be the realisation that basic science is and always will be the fountain of knowledge on which improved diagnoses and treatments are based. The focus on patients is not to compete against basic science, it is a mind-set and establishment of the research structure that integrates basic science faster and more completely with translation, moving the knowledge into health products or improved health care as efficiently as possible.

Brain research is completed in individuals with disorders, who are first diagnosed and treated by individual clinicians. The role of clinicians in the proposed approach to research is critically important. Samuel Volchenboum, Director of Informatics, University of Chicago, said that without clinical data, information derived from other platforms such as genetics, is deprived of much of its importance (Asadi, 2013). Moreover, the number of patients entered into the data base increases the value for big data analyses. The importance is recognised – but in many, if not most, health systems, clinicians are reimbursed for their work by the number of patients they see. Being involved in research protocols minimises their financial gain, because of the extra time required to perform each evaluation in a truly standardised manner and then enter the data in the informatics system. Big data requires a continual flow of new data, normally gathered by the clinician, even if through ordering a specific evaluation. What is the rationale for a clinician to be involved? There has to be mechanisms of compensating for clinician involvement, if their salary is dependent on the number of patients they see, either by supplementing their salary or providing the methods to make the research involvement a seamless part of their daily work; e.g., patient co-ordinator, easy-to-use data management platforms, and automated data capture.

Most important is patient engagement. Individuals with brain disorders are the key from virtually every aspect. Without them, there are no data, there are no clinical trials. Without them, there is no research. Public confidence in the value and process of sharing data is essential for this to succeed (Walker et al., 2014). A major risk, then, occurs when patients are "research subjects" and not partners. They must be partners in both the process and the outcomes. Results must be fully shared. As rapid as possible implementation of results is the most important win for patients. As such, commercialisation to develop products from research (medications and technologies), knowledge exchange and translation, changes in health care delivery and policy – each is an important outcome for patient involvement.

Another key topic is security and privacy which is an evolving landscape and with rapid advances in imaging, genomics and data sharing methods, it is becoming increasingly important to ensure appropriate mechanisms for the storage, processing, and disclosure of data, in particular as we contemplate the sharing of data across institutions, regions, and borders. This evolving landscape significantly influences other processes, such as ethics consent forms. International standards need to be established and accepted.

5.7. Next steps

We recommend a series of action items to facilitate the development of the information superhighway and data sharing.

- Big data for AD and dementia need to move from silos to systems. Many initiatives are occurring world-wide with many different groups focusing on different disorders. Dialogue should be initiated among leaders of such major big data initiatives (e.g., One Mind for Research; Global Alliance for Genomics and Health; GAAIN; IMI; JPND; OBI; CEOi GAP; company-specific programmes) to develop common governance policies and practices. In turn, this could lead to collaborations for evaluating many different types of large datasets not normally used together for addressing major current challenges in AD and dementia. For example, it could lead to new collaborative efforts to identify, develop and validate AD biomarkers that combine imaging, clinical, genomic, and other relevant information.

- Realising the promise of big data requires broad and sustained public trust. Efforts, therefore, need to include a focus on privacy, responsible informed consent policies, personal engagement, and updated legislation and regulatory regimes.
  - Big data demands big privacy (Cavoukian et al., 2014). Policies may vary between jurisdictions. It is essential to examine differences and commonalities in privacy practices internationally, and adopt a common privacy approach. A formal declaration, and then acceptance by institution and university CEOs, would be an important step forward. This includes harmonisation of ethics processes, including consent forms.
  - Consistent, broad, standardised and enduring consent needs to become a building block for all prospective studies.
  - New governance mechanisms should be evaluated to ensure an environment favorable to the widespread use, diffusion, and access to big data through legislation, regulations, and other means.
- Sustainability of databases has to be addressed. Khachaturian (2013) has suggested a call to action for the global community to create an inventory of existing resources as part of the solution. Awareness at the government level is needed to ensure adequate continuing resources. At the same time, new business models for establishing, curating, financing, and maintaining sustainable large datasets and cohorts need to be evaluated and developed.
- It is important to organise and launch a demonstration of feasibility of sharing of data. This also needs to include consideration of the full range of different types of data, especially methods, standards, interoperability, and metadata.
- Priority also should be given to avoiding data "silos" and taking advantage of the full power enabled by big data and new data analytics tools by linking large-scale research datasets to: 1) clinical health records and routine health records; 2) environmental and socio-economic datasets; and 3) clinical trial data. For example, prototype collaborations might be developed to identify sub-populations "at risk" of AD and dementia by using existing datasets that span the full range of research, clinical, and environmental datasets.

Note

1. This chapter has been written by: Donald T. Stuss, PhD, Ontario Brain Institute, Toronto, Canada; Shiva Amiri, PhD, Ontario Brain Institute, Toronto, Canada; Martin Rossor, MD, University College London, United Kingdom; Richard Johnson, M.S., J.D., CEO, Global Helix LLC; Zaven Khachaturian, PhD, Alzheimer's Association, United States.

References

Asadi, N.B. (2013), "Industry Voices: Inside Genomics Q&A with Bina CEO Narges Bani Asadi and Sam Volchenboum", Fierce Biotech, Nov. 7, available from www.fiercebiotech.com/story/industry-voices-inside-genomics-qa-bina-ceo-narges-bani-asadi-and-sam-volch/2013-11-07.

Barnes, D.E., K. Yaffe, N. Belfor, W.J. Jagust, C. DeCarli, B.R. Reed et al. (2009), "Computer-based Cognitive Training for Mild Cognitive Impairment: Results from a Pilot Randomized, Controlled Trial", *Alzheimer Disease and Associated Disorders*, Vol. 23, No. 3, pp. 205-210.

Callaway, E. (2012), "Alzheimer's Drugs Take a New Tack", *Nature*, Vol. 489, pp. 13-14.

Cavoukian, A. and D. Reed (2013), "Big Privacy: Bridging Big Data and the Personal Data Ecosystem Through '*Privacy By Design*'", Information Privacy Commissioner, Toronto, December, available from www.ipc.on.ca/images/Resources/pbd-big_privacy.pdf.

Cavoukian, A., D. Steward and B. Dewitt (2014), "Using *Privacy by Design* to Achieve Big Data Innovation Without Compromising Privacy", Information Privacy Commissioner, Toronto, June, available from www.privacybydesign.ca/content/uploads/2014/06/pbd-big-data-innovation_Deloitte.pdf.

Craik, F.I., E. Bialystok and M. Freedman (2010), "Delaying the Onset of Alzheimer Disease: Bilingualism as a Form of Cognitive Reserve", *Neurology*, Vol. 75, No. 19, pp. 1726-1729.

Cukier, K.N. and V. Mayer-Schoenberger (2013), "The Rise of Big Data: How It's Changing the Way We Think About the World", Foreign Affairs [Internet], April 3, available from www.foreignaffairs.com/articles/139104/kenneth-neil-cukier-and-viktor-mayer-schoenberger/the-rise-of-big-data.

Data Protection and Privacy Commissioners, 32nd International Conference – Resolution on Privacy by Design: www.justice.gov.il/NR/rdonlyres/F8A79347-170C-4EEF-A0AD-155554558A5F/26502/ResolutiononPrivacybyDesign.pdf.

Eichler, H.-G., F. Petavy, F. Pignatti and G. Rasi (2013), "Access to Patient-level Trial Data – A Boon to Drug Developers", *New England Journal of Medicine*, Vol. 369, No. 17, pp. 1577-1579.

Georgiades, S., P. Szatmari, M. Boyle, S. Hanna, E. Duku, L. Zwaigenbaum et al. (2013), "Investigating Phenotypic Heterogeneity in Children with Autism Spectrum Disorder: A Factor Mixture Modeling Approach", Journal of Child Psychology and Psychiatry, Vol. 54, No. 2, pp. 206-215.

JPND Research News, available from www.neurodegenerationresearch.eu/news-events/research-news/research-news-article/?no_cache=1&tx_ttnews%5Btt_news%5D=118&cHash=8789af6f5a78dc365ef1af87d7079872

Khachaturian, A.S. (2013), "Big Data, Aging, and Dementia: Pathways for International Harmonization on Data Sharing", *Alzheimer's and Dementia*, Vol. 9, pp. 261-262.

Khachaturian, Z.S. (2012), "Perspectives on Alzheimer's Disease: Past, Present and Future", in M.C. Carrillo and H. Hampel (eds.), *Alzheimer's Disease – Modernising Concept, Biological Diagnosis and Therapy, Advances in Biological Psychiatry*, Karger, Basel, pp. 179-188.

Institute of Medicine (2008), *From Molecules to Minds: Challenges for the 21st Century: Workshop Summary,* National Academies Press, Washington, DC.

National Research Council (2014), "Discussion Framework for Clinical Trial Data Sharing: Guiding Principles, Elements, and Activities", Washington, DC.

National Research Council of the National Academies (2011), "Toward Precision Medicine: Building a Knowledge Network for Biomedical Research and a New Taxonomy of Disease", Washington, DC.

OECD (2014), "Unleashing the Power of Information Communication Technologies and Big Data Towards a Roadmap for International Action", Main points from the OECD Expert Consultation on "Unlocking Global Collaboration to Accelerate Innovation for Alzheimer's Disease and Dementia"; Oxford, United Kingdom, available from www.oecd-ilibrary.org/science-and-technology/unleashing-the-power-of-big-data-for-alzheimer-s-disease-and-dementia-research_5jz73kvmvbwb-en?crawler=true.

OECD (2013a), "Progress Report on the Project to Strengthen Health Information Infrastructure. Patient Experiences Subgroup Meeting and HCQI Expert Group Meeting", Nov. 7-8, Paris.

OECD (2013b), "Unleashing the Power of Information Communication Technologies and Big Data", *Issues Paper 2,* prepared for the OECD Expert Consultation on Unlocking Global Collaboration to Accelerate Innovation for Alzheimer's Disease and Dementia, Jun 20-21, Oxford, United Kingdom.

OECD (2013c), "Emerging Trends in Biomedicine and Health Technology Innovation: Addressing the Global Challenge of Alzheimer's", *OECD Science, Technology and Industry Policy Papers*, No. 6, OECD Publishing, Paris, http://dx.doi.org/10.1787/5k44zcpt65vc-en.

Ontario Brain Institute (2013). "The Role of Physical Activity in the Prevention and Management of Alzheimer's Disease – Implications for Ontario", 25 Feb., available from www.braininstitute.ca/sites/default/files/final_report_obi_pa_alzheimers_february_25_2013.pdf

Poline, J.-P., J.L. Breeze, S. Ghosh, K. Gorgolewski, Y.O. Halchenko, M. Hanke et al. (2012), "Data Sharing in Neuroimaging Research", *Frontiers in Neuroinformatics*, Vol. 6, pp. 1-13.

Rosen, A.C., L. Sugiura, J.H. Kramer and J.D. Whitfield-Gabrieli (2011), "Cognitive Training Changes Hippocampal Function in Mild Cognitive Impairment: A Pilot Study", *Journal of Alzheimer's Disease*, Vol. 26, No. 3, pp. 349-357.

Stern, Y. (2012), "Cognitive Reserve in Ageing and Alzheimer's Disease", *The Lancet Neurology*, Vol. 11, No. 11, pp. 1006-1012.

Stuss, D.T. (2014), "The Ontario Brain Institute: Completing the Cycle", *Canadian Journal of Neurological Sciences*, forthcoming.

Stuss, D.T. and M.A. Binns (2008), "The Patient as a Moving Target: The Importance to Rehabilitation of Understanding Variability", in D.T. Stuss, G. Winocur and I.H. Robertson (eds.), *Cognitive Neurorehabilitation*, 2nd Edition: Evidence and Application, Cambridge University Press, pp. 39-61.

Taylor, N.P. (2014), "Europe's Brain Project Plans Grant Incentives to Encourage Data Sharing", *Fierce BiotechIT*, Jun. 30, available from: www.fiercebiotechit.com/story/europes-brain-project-plans-grant-incentives-encourage-data-sharing/2014-06-30

Walker, P., J. Meikle and R. Ramesh (2014), "NHS in England Delays Sharing of Medical Records", *The Guardian*. Feb. 18, available from www.theguardian.com/society/2014/feb/18/nhs-delays-sharing-medical-records-care-data.

Wilhelm, E.E., E. Oster and I. Shoulson (2014), "Approaches and Costs for Sharing Clinical Research Data", *Journal of American Medical Association*, Mar. 26, Vol. 311, No. 12, pp. 1201-1202, available from http://jama.jamanetwork.com/article.aspx?articleID=1833396.

Chapter 6

Governing health data access and privacy: OECD experiences

Jillian Oderkirk[1]

Data that describes health care pathways and outcomes is a key element of the broad data needed to be part of an international strategy around big data and dementia. Effective collaboration of health ministries, justice ministries and data privacy regulators is required if the societal benefits from the use of these data are to be maximised and the privacy risks minimised. OECD conducted surveys to better understand the use and governance of these data in different countries. The surveys showed important differences across jurisdictions and identified key governance factors. The chapter concludes that governments should share best practices in data governance and norms for accrediting data processors. It highlights the importance of reviewing legal frameworks for protection of personal health information privacy, the nature of patient consent and data security risks and mechanisms to mitigate them. The paper emphasizes the need to explore mechanisms to engage the public in the discussion about benefits of these data and the commitment to data privacy and the rights of data subjects.

6.1. Introduction

OECD countries are ageing and increasing shares of our populations are living longer with multiple chronic and disabling conditions. Dementias, in particular, are prevalent and complex conditions and dementia patients require care from multiple providers as they are frequently elderly, suffering from multiple chronic conditions and in need of community care assistance as well as health care services. Effectively co-ordinating care and ensuring high quality care for dementia patients is a priority.

The rising prevalence of chronic health conditions, including dementias, has important implications for how care is best organised and provided; where new treatment innovations can be expected; and future cost pressures on governments. To address the burden of chronic conditions, medicine must focus on preventing their onset and on controlling their progression. At the same time, health systems must focus on improvements in care quality and co-ordination; and efficient care delivery and on finding new ways to make systems more productive and sustainable.

Better data will be needed to assess and compare the effectiveness of therapies and services provided to chronically ill patients. Better data will also be needed to support re-designing and evaluating new models of health care service delivery and to contribute to the discovery and evaluation of new treatments. The health data needed, however, is often both personal and sensitive, and protection of the privacy of data subjects is required. Decision making about potential statistical or research uses of personal health data should include consideration of both the societal risks and benefits from the data use. If both dimensions are not evaluated, then decision making is likely to be sub-optimal for society.

Health ministry leadership is necessary to ensure that delivering the data to manage this important sector is at the forefront of government policy and action. Effective collaboration between health ministries, justice ministries and data privacy regulators is essential if governments are to evolve toward a situation where societal benefits from data use are maximised and risks to society from data use are minimised. At the same time, government needs clear and open channels to engage with stakeholders in the development and use of data, so that data governance frameworks and practices reflect societal values and priorities.

While all countries are investing in data infrastructure, there are significant cross-country differences in data availability and use, with some countries standing out with significant progress and innovative practices enabling privacy-respectful data use, and others falling behind with insufficient data and restrictions that limit access to and use of data, even by government itself (OECD, 2013a). To support OECD countries in improving data governance frameworks, the OECD is investigating the legal frameworks, policies and practices that are in place to protect the privacy of data subjects when data is being processed and analysed. The purpose of this investigation is to understand the current situation, uncover and document practices, and make recommendations of promising data governance practices that enable privacy-respectful monitoring and research. This paper summarises the benefits and risks associated with high-value health data; describes the variability across countries in data availability and use; introduces a data governance framework to maximise societal benefits from data use while minimising societal risks; and describes promising data governance mechanisms. The chapter concludes with international actions that can support countries in strengthening data governance.

6.2. High-value data describes health care pathways and outcomes

Essential to health care quality and performance assessment is the ability to track patients as they progress back and forth through the health care system from primary health care to speciality care to hospitalisations, long-term care, home care, and hospice care. This data should also provide information about underlying patient characteristics, illnesses, medications, therapies, tests and images, and deaths. This type of follow-up permits a comprehensive view of health care services provided and the health outcomes of those services; and permits uncovering medical errors, adverse drug reactions, fraud, adherence to clinical guidelines, effective treatments, optimal care paths and optimal responders to treatment (OECD, 2013a, 2014).

Understanding pathways often requires linking datasets at the patient level, as current health data are usually collected in silos, such as primary health care datasets, datasets of in-patient hospitalisations, long-term care datasets, disease registries, pharmaceutical datasets and death registries.

The capacity to construct accurate data to assess pathways, outcomes and costs is increasing rapidly as health care systems adopt and use information technologies. The use of data from electronic health records (EHRs), in particular, has the potential to enable a quantum leap in health care quality and performance assessment because such records can be become part of an electronic health record system that captures patients' health care pathways and outcomes.

Health data use puts patients' privacy at risk

Historically, a duty to honour confidentiality has arisen with respect to information disclosed in the context of a confidential relationship, such as that between an individual and his or her physician, attorney, or priest. In such relationships, the confidante is under an obligation not to disclose the information learned in the course of the relationship. Now the law applies such duties to holders of information who do not have a confidential relationship to a patient, but where the data held is detailed enough to identify the data subjects.

Health data that can be linked to measure pathways and outcomes is often both personal and sensitive. It is personal because there is information that identifies individuals and it is sensitive because it includes aspects of individual's health and health care treatments and services that they have received. In many cases, the data is an outcome of the confidential relationship between patients and their health care providers. Both the sharing and the linkage of such data risk the protection of the privacy of the persons whose data is involved. When data is shared it may be lost or stolen during the transfer process, or the data recipient may not provide sufficient protection to keep the data confidential. When data is linked, the combined dataset provides more information about the data subjects than did the original unlinked datasets. Thus, the resulting linked data could cause more harm to data subjects if it were lost, stolen or otherwise misused.

Half of countries link data regularly to monitor quality and performance

Most OECD countries have large national datasets that would support regular data linkage to monitor health care quality and system performance (OECD, 2013a). Only a minority, however, are exercising that opportunity (Figure 6.1).

In 2011/12, twelve of nineteen countries were regularly linking hospital data and mortality data, and eleven were regularly linking cancer registry data. This number drops considerably for other national databanks – with only a handful of countries regularly benefiting from their data to improve health care quality on a national level, such as Belgium, Denmark, Finland, Israel, Korea, Portugal, and Sweden.

Figure 6.1. All 19 countries have national data, but few regularly link the data to report on health care quality

Number of countries

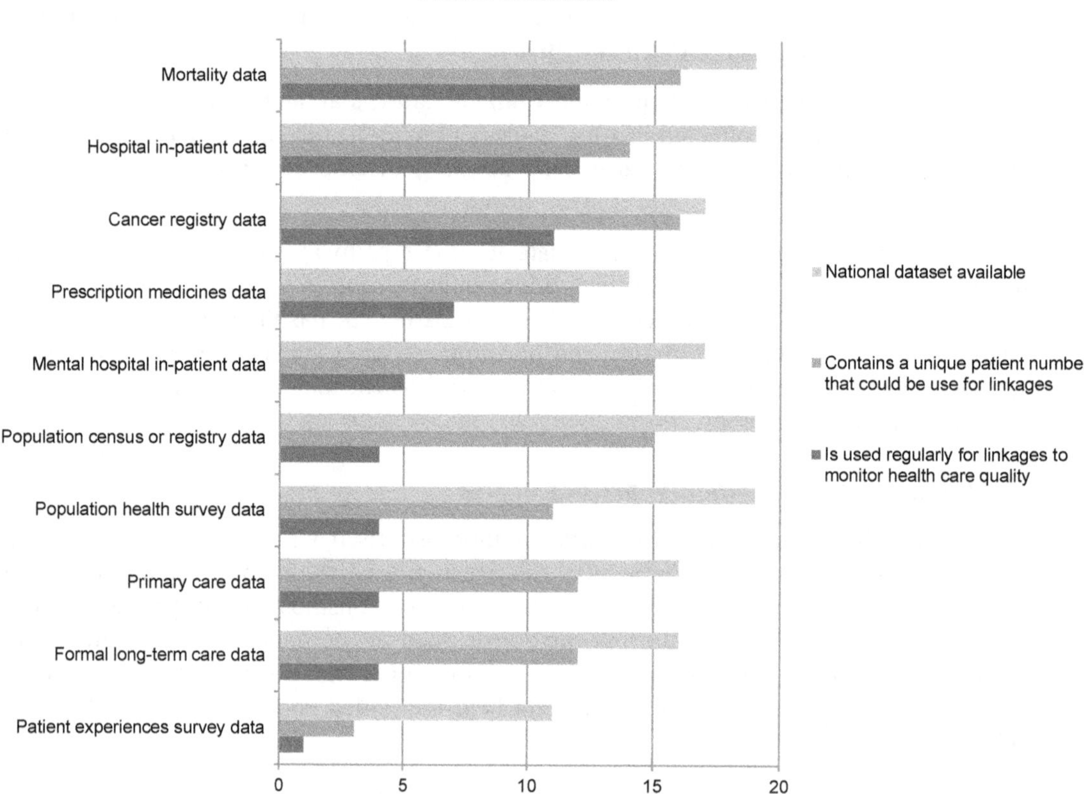

Source: OECD HCQI Country Survey, 2011/12.

Countries are developing data from electronic health record systems

The development and use of data from electronic health records is essential to realising the power of patient data to improve the quality, safety and performance of health care systems. Progress toward EHR systems began with moving clinicians and hospitals toward electronic record keeping. In 2012, twelve of 25 countries reported that 80% or more of their primary care physician offices and hospitals capture patient diagnosis and treatment electronically (OECD, 2013a).

Electronic health record systems, as we defined them, are systems of electronic records of patients that contain or virtually link together records from multiple health care providers creating a longitudinal view of the patient's health care history or treatment pathway.

Most countries reported a national plan or policy to implement an electronic health record system (22 of 25 countries) and most had already begun to implement that plan by 2012 (20 countries). At that time, the implementation was relatively new in virtually all participating countries, having started within the previous four years. Of the twenty-five countries studied, eighteen countries included some form of secondary analysis of electronic health records within their national plan (Figure 6.2). The most commonly included secondary uses reported by fifteen countries were public health monitoring and health system performance monitoring. Fourteen countries also indicated that they intended for physicians to be able to query the data to support treatment decisions. The least commonly-reported planned data use was for facilitating or contributing to clinical trials. This use was noted by ten countries.

Many countries also reported that regular use of electronic health record data for secondary analyses were already underway. Public health monitoring (13 countries) and general research (11 countries) were the most commonly reported uses.

There are differences between the thirteen countries whose national plans or policies called for at least four of the data uses outlined in Figure 6.2 (the keen) and the twelve countries who were planning on fewer or no secondary data uses (the reluctant) (OECD, 2015a). Keen countries were Belgium, Estonia, Finland, France, Indonesia, Korea, Mexico, Poland, Portugal, Singapore, Slovak Republic, the United Kingdom and the United States.

The majority of keen countries (69%) are implementing an EHR system that will enable the sharing of records between and among physicians and hospitals, and that will include information on current medications, lab tests and medical images. In contrast, none of the reluctant countries are implementing an EHR system with all of these features. Further, virtually all of the keen countries (92%) have developed a national minimum data set that standardises the content of patient records that are intended to be shared among health care providers. In contrast, only one-half of the reluctant countries have defined a minimum data set. The majority of keen countries, 62%, reported that all or most of the key data elements within their EHR (diagnosis, medications, lab tests, medical images and surgical procedures) follow clinical terminology standards. In contrast, only 17% of reluctant countries have adopted clinical terminology standards to the same degree.

Keen countries (54%) are somewhat more likely than reluctant countries (42%) to report that their EHR system is already being used to create datasets for secondary analysis. Keen countries are much more likely than reluctant countries to have put into place processes to evaluate the usability of EHR data for statistical purposes (69%, compared with 17%). As a result, it is perhaps not surprising that keen countries (62%) are more likely than reluctant countries (50%) to be concerned with the quality of the data being entered into electronic clinical records. Keen countries (31%), compared with reluctant countries (17%), are also more likely to have instituted processes for auditing the clinical content of electronic records for quality.

Figure 6.2. Planned and implemented uses of data from electronic health record systems in 25 OECD countries

Number of countries

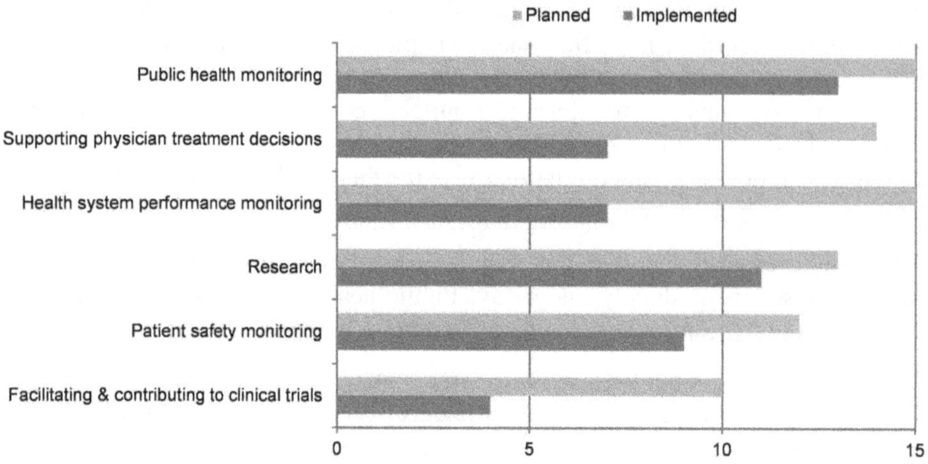

Planned Implemented

Public health monitoring
Supporting physician treatment decisions
Health system performance monitoring
Research
Patient safety monitoring
Facilitating & contributing to clinical trials

0 5 10 15

Source: OECD HCQI Country Survey, 2012.

6.3. Optimal decision making requires a data governance framework that maximises societal benefits and minimises societal risks

The overarching framework for the OECD investigation in 2013-14 is that decision making about potential statistical or research uses of personal health data should be taken after considering both societal risks from the data use and societal benefits from the data use (Figure 6.3). Figure 6.3 outlines factors that should influence decision making about a potential use of personal health data. The centre of the figure is the proposed data use. Flanking the proposed data use are its potential benefits (on the left) and its potential risks (on the right).

To illustrate the point, examples of benefits are shown on the right, such as individual's rights to health; respect of societal values toward health and safe, efficient and effective health care; direct benefits to patients' health and health care; and benefits to the health system from efficiency and innovation.

Examples of risks are shown on the left including violating individual's rights to privacy; diminishing societal trust in government and health care providers; disrespecting societal values regarding privacy and data sharing; harming patients including lost privacy, discrimination and identity theft; and harming health care systems including lost privacy, decreased trust and lost market share.

The second important dimension of this framework is data governance. Optimal decision making about potential statistical and research uses of data can only be achieved if there is an overarching data governance framework in the country that has itself been optimised to minimise societal risks from data use and to maximise societal benefits from data use. In Figure 6.3, the arrows on the right and left of the diagram illustrate the data governance mechanisms that can increase societal benefits and reduce societal risks from data use.

Figure 6.3. Data-use decisions should be made by weighing societal benefits and risks within a data governance framework that maximises benefits and minimises risks

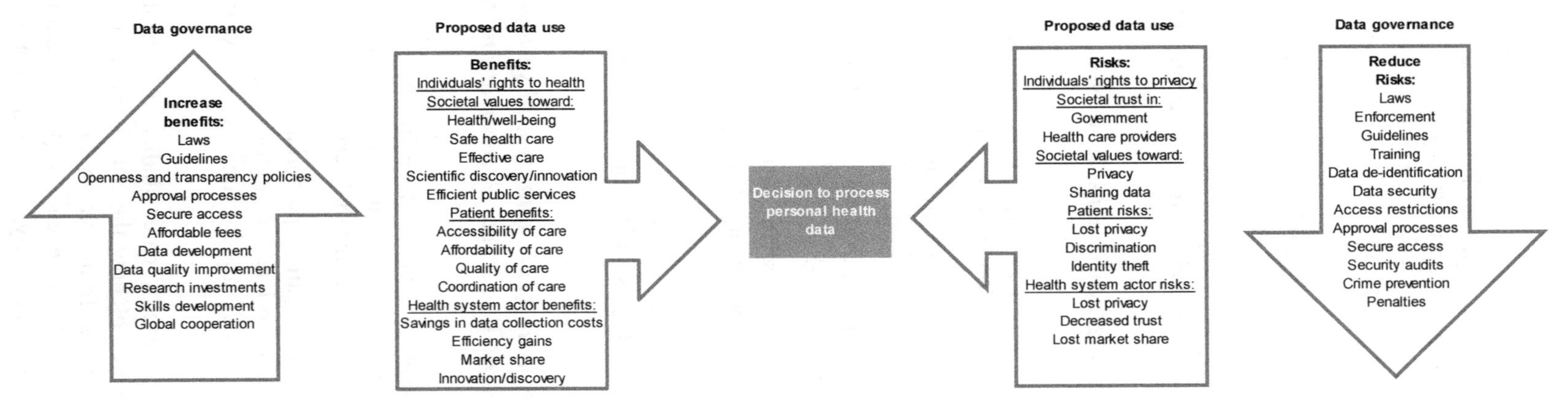

Source: OECD (2015), "Governing Personal Health Data for Health Care Quality, Health System Performance and Research Innovation: Mechanisms and Tools for Privacy-Respectful Data Use" (working title), OECD Health Policy Studies, Paris, forthcoming.

6.4. Eight governance factors maximising societal benefits of data use while minimising societal risks

In 2013, 22 countries completed a detailed questionnaire regarding their data assets and how they are governed. These countries also identified key national experts in the legal framework for the protection of health information privacy and in aspects of the governance of health data who were then interviewed. Initial analysis of the results of this study point to the following key factors supporting maximising societal benefits and minimising risks:[2]

- The health information system supports health care quality and system performance monitoring and improvement, and research innovations for better health care and outcomes.
- The public are consulted upon and informed about the collection and processing of personal health data.
- Data subjects have reasonable and practical means to express their choices regarding the use of their data.
- The sharing of data for research and statistical purposes is permitted, subject to suitable safeguards set up by the data protection legislative framework.
- Data is concentrated within accredited data custodians meeting high standards for data governance.
- The project approval process is fair and transparent and decisions are taken with input from an independent project approval body.
- Best practices in data de-identification and secure data access are applied to protect patient data privacy without compromising data utility or fair access to data.
- Governance mechanisms are periodically reviewed to maximise societal benefits and minimise societal risks as new data sources and new technologies are introduced.

The health information system supports health care quality and system performance monitoring and improvement, and research innovations for better health care and outcomes

Health data collected by national governments that can be linked and shared is a valuable resource that can be used to improve the health outcomes of dementia patients and the quality and performance of the health care systems that serve them.

It makes ethical sense to use this data to its fullest potential within a governance framework that minimises risks to data subjects' privacy. Countries that have developed strong health data governance frameworks provide good examples of how data can be used safely to benefit society.

Countries that are actively monitoring health care quality and health system performance provide very interesting examples of how the data is being used and the benefits accrued. Examples of data use range from evaluation of the quality and cost-effectiveness of treatments to monitoring adverse events related to pharmaceuticals and medical devices; to incorporating results of analysis of care pathways within evaluations of and revisions to clinical care guidelines; to building pathway data to promote world-class research (see references). While very few of these examples focus on dementia patients, the techniques could be applied to dementia-related monitoring and research. Leading countries include Canada, Denmark, Finland, Israel, Korea, New Zealand, Singapore, Sweden and the United Kingdom (England, Scotland and Wales).

The public are consulted upon and informed about the collection and processing of personal health data

Public awareness is often limited regarding the data inputs to the health information system, the users of the system, the uses of the system, the benefits and risks that are associated with the system and their rights with respect to their own data. Communicating about uses of and safeguards surrounding personal health data is both challenging and essential to public trust and confidence in governments.

Twelve countries have a policy or programme in place to promote open government health data to increase transparency in and access to aggregated health statistics. Countries rarely, however, provide the public with a centralised location where they can inform themselves about all of the national health datasets, and, in particular, the national personal health datasets.

Some countries provide the public with information regarding approved studies involving the processing of personal health data including dataset linkages. No countries reported informing the public about applications for approval to process personal health data. Increasing transparency about data processing would improve public awareness of and engagement in health data governance.

The United Kingdom provided several examples about efforts to consult the public about data governance; involve the public in decision making about data governance; and inform the public about data use, safeguards and their rights. The United Kingdom also provided examples of lessons-learned when public communication has not been effective (National Health Service, 2014).

Data subjects have reasonable and practical means to express their choices regarding the use of their data

The secondary analysis of personal health data is typically permitted in countries with the consent of the data subject or when the analysis has been legally authorised. Informed consent presumes the ability to indicate clearly to a participant the use of their data and the purpose of a particular research activity. This is feasible for a purpose-specific study, such as an invitation to patients to participate in a clinical trial or a survey. The requirement to obtain patient consent presents significant challenges, however, for health and health care monitoring and research involving large population and patient databases. These databases are collected for other purposes, such as administering the health system or providing clinical care and represent hundreds of thousands to millions of persons. In some cases, such as the development of biobanks, the purpose of the collection is to support future research.

The future uses of health data collected today depend upon decisions taken regarding conditions where there may be exemptions to consent requirements and on whether or not it is possible to ask individuals to consent to uses of their data in the future that cannot be specified in a detailed way. Such broad consent does not imply that there is no further governance of data uses, as decisions about specific data uses can be governed by designated authorities, such as independent research ethics boards or data privacy regulators. Opt-out consent models in the United Kingdom and Sweden enable individuals to express their choice regarding future uses of data about them that is within administrative and clinical datasets or biobanks that can be administered in a practical manner. Countries developing a portal where patients can access their own clinical records, such as Iceland and Finland, could use the portal to enable patients to express their choice about the use of their data for statistics and research.

The sharing of data for research and statistical purposes is permitted, subject to suitable safeguards set up by the data protection legislative framework

Custodians of national health data in Denmark, New Zealand, Finland, Sweden, and the United Kingdom indicated that the sharing of identifiable data may be permitted for research or statistical purposes subject to approval processes and data security controls. In these countries, the same rules apply to applicants from the government sector, the academic or non-profit sector and the commercial sector, provided the purpose of use is research or statistics. In other countries, most or all identifiable national data may only be shared with consent or where there is a specific legal authorisation.

National data custodians in several countries will review applications for access to de-identified data for research or statistics from all sectors of society (Denmark, Finland, Korea, Switzerland and the United Kingdom). In some countries, however, applications from commercial entities are restricted or prohibited [Canada, Iceland, the United Kingdom (Wales) and the United States]. There were also custodians reporting that de-identified person-level data is never shared but, there are secure alternatives to data sharing that enable statistical and research projects to take place (Canada, Netherlands, Japan, Korea, Singapore, the United Kingdom and the United States). These secure access mechanisms are rarely available to applicants from the commercial sector.

European countries participating in this study have a clear and similar interpretation of data sharing requirements with foreign entities. If data is identifiable or it is de-identified but still carries a re-identification risk, then the data privacy protection legislation in the applicant's country must be evaluated as providing adequate protection of data subject's privacy.

Country experts reported data sharing challenges including legal prohibitions to national statistical authorities sharing identifiable personal health data with health ministries; and slow and sometimes unsuccessful negotiations of data sharing agreements among national data custodians. A lack of legal or regulatory obligations for health care providers to contribute data to national statistics is an obstacle, particularly for national data about primary health care. There are also legal or policy constraints to extracting data from electronic clinical record systems in some countries.

Data is concentrated within accredited data custodians meeting high standards for data governance

Countries with concentrated custodianship of national data can conduct data linkage projects without entering into negotiations and data sharing agreements with other data holders. Thus they are more likely to have regular programmes to monitor health and health care quality and performance that are based on data following the pathway of care. They are also larger and more likely to be resourced to develop staff with the technical skills and knowledge of data quality and limitations to enable efficient data processing. They are also able to better serve external data users through more transparent communication about data availability and accessibility, more timely approval processes, more useful data access mechanisms, and less costly processing. Seventy-percent or more of the key national datasets of personal health information are held by a single organisation in the Czech Republic, Denmark, Iceland, Japan, New Zealand, Sweden, Switzerland, Turkey, the United States and the United Kingdom (England, Scotland and Wales).

An accreditation or certification process can narrow the number of processors to only those who meet the country's highest standards for data privacy and security protection. Further, follow-up audits can ensure that these standards are maintained. Accreditation of data processors is under consideration in England and the Health and Social Care Information Centre already has the features of an accredited safe haven. Within Scotland there are currently five accredited safe havens. Australia has implemented accreditation and the Australian Institute for Health and Welfare, which is the national health ministry, has been accredited.

The project approval process is fair and transparent and decisions are taken with input from an independent project approval body

Fair and transparent project approval processes are essential to meeting public expectations regarding appropriate uses of their personal health data. Elements of a fair and transparent process include the independence of project reviewers from those seeking or realising a benefit from a project; the degree to which the public is informed about the existence of, the members of and role of project reviewers; and the degree to which national authorities are open about the process that must be followed to apply for and be approved access to data, including data from record linkage processes.

Independent research ethics review boards advise data custodians on proposals involving the processing of personal health data in Israel, Sweden, New Zealand, the United Kingdom and the United States. Data custodians have established internal review committees that have a mix of both internal and external experts in Japan, Korea and the United States. The data protection regulator takes the final decision on project approval with advice from research ethics boards and custodians in Denmark and Iceland. The data privacy regulator is consulted in Finland, Switzerland and the Czech Republic.

Nine countries indicated that there is public information, such as a website where the process for requesting access to de-identified data and the process to request a dataset linkage are described for all of the key national health datasets (the Czech Republic, Iceland, Korea, New Zealand, Norway, Sweden, the United States and the United Kingdom) or for the majority (Canada, Netherlands and Finland). Five countries are fully transparent about applications for access to de-identified data but, conversely, do not provide information about the record linkage process for all or most key health datasets [Denmark, Ireland, Switzerland, the United Kingdom (Wales), and Japan].

Best practices in data de-identification and secure data access are applied to protect patient data privacy without compromising data utility or fair access to data

Data is de-identified when it does not identify individuals directly and it cannot reasonably be used to determine individuals' identities. However, rarely will data de-identification processes reduce the risk to zero that an individual could be identified from person-level data. Data de-identification must be part of a broader set of data security mechanisms.

De-identification processes

In many countries, direct identifiers are suppressed when data is provided for analysis. In eleven countries, pseudonyms are created from direct identifiers within all or most key national health datasets before they are made available for analysis. In this technique, identifying information about individuals is converted to a meaningless name or number in a consistent manner. The consistency of the application of the pseudonymisation algorithm permits record linkage among datasets for approved projects.

Data masking refers to a set of methods used to modify dataset variables in order to reduce the likelihood that they could be used to re-identify the data. Common techniques include releasing only partial dates, such as month and year but not day; larger geographies, such as postal code districts rather than exact postal codes; and broad categories such as primary, secondary or tertiary care. Sometimes "noise" is added to the data, such as swapping values among dataset records with similar characteristics, rounding values, or otherwise distorting original values. Data treatment can be so extensive that public dissemination of detailed data is possible (public-use micro data and micro-aggregate data).

Decisions made about data de-identification need to consider "the big picture". Data suppression and masking techniques can have detrimental impacts on the ability to conduct certain studies or on the validity of study findings. Several countries reported that the utility of the data for its intended purpose is a factor in decision making about data de-identification processes. The United States and the United Kingdom provided examples of how decision making about data de-identification processes are taken within a broader context of the data security measures that may be in place.

Data security mechanisms

Data security mechanisms include basic governance of the physical and IT security of data processors; as well as data access controls and staff training; and secure channels for data transmission. They also include signed obligations such as contracts and data sharing agreements that bind data recipients to the rules which protect the data. All of these basic mechanisms are widely used in OECD countries.

In England, a custodian described how a data requestor's data security environment is assessed before data access is granted. The evaluation is particularly strict if access to identifiable data may be granted and a follow-up audit may be conducted to confirm compliance after approval. A custodian in Canada described that signed agreements include provisions for an external follow-up audit to ensure compliance. Other custodians have a telephone follow-up with data recipients.

Countries universally observe that researchers have a strong incentive to comply with the terms of data sharing agreements because any misuse of data could damage their career. Some countries impose a fine or criminal conviction for deliberate misuse of data (Korea, the United Kingdom, and statistical authorities in Canada and the United States).

Secure research data centres and secure remote data access systems are viable alternatives to transferring person-level data to data requestors. These secure facilities are effective at both broadening access to data and reducing the risk that data could be lost or misused. Secure research data centres are used in Canada, Japan, Singapore, the Netherlands and the United States. Remote data access systems offering researchers real-time service and the ability to conduct sophisticated data modelling with appropriate software are available in the United Kingdom (Scotland and Wales), the Netherlands and the United States. Such an environment is undergoing pilot testing in Korea and is in development in Denmark.

Governance mechanisms are periodically reviewed to maximise societal benefits and minimise societal risks as new data sources and new technologies are introduced

Best practices in data governance require continual assessment and renewal. This is because the volume, velocity and variety of health data is growing rapidly and the technologies used to communicate, process and store data are evolving. Further, legal frameworks continue to be renewed to reflect societal values and address requirements of a changing health information landscape. Ongoing collaboration among stakeholders in the development and use of health data is essential to developing balanced policy decisions that can reach the goal of maximising societal benefits and minimising societal risks.

6.5. Next steps at the international level

The results of the 2013/14 OECD study highlighted here are being analysed to develop a set of recommended data governance mechanisms to assist countries in strengthening their health information infrastructure. This work includes a taxonomy of risks and benefits that countries can apply to support decision making about proposed data development and uses. Continued international collaboration in this dynamic area is essential for information about best practices and lessons learned in health data governance to circulate widely; also to support harmonisation toward common best practices, so that multi-country statistical and research projects are feasible. There are particular areas revealed in this study where international collaboration is needed. These include:

- Monitoring national implementation of best practices in data governance, such as these eight recommended data governance mechanisms.
- Supporting countries in developing the norms necessary for governments to certify or accredit data processors.
- Supporting countries in evaluating which national legal frameworks for the protection of health information privacy provide adequate protections to facilitate multi-country statistical and research projects.
- Reviewing current practices in patient consent and in waivers to consent and reaching a common understanding about mechanisms that are privacy respectful.
- Reviewing developments in data security risks and threats and mechanisms to address them.
- Exploring mechanisms to engage the public in discussion about data and its governance and to ensure there is good public awareness of health data, the benefits of its use, its protection, and the rights of data subjects.

Notes

1. This chapter has been written by Jillian Oderkirk, OECD.
2. The results of the 2013/14 study presented in this paper are preliminary and are subject to on-going review by OECD countries and their experts in law and health data governance. Final results are planned for 2015. All errors are the responsibility of the author.

References

Canadian Institute for health Information (2012), *Pathways of Care for People with Stroke in Ontario*, Ottawa, https://secure.cihi.ca/free_products/Pathways_of_care_aib_en.pdf accessed 7 August 2014.

Cancer Research UK (2013), "ICBP Publications", www.cancerresearchuk.org/cancer-info/spotcancerearly/ICBP/icbp-publications/ accessed 14 September 2013.

Coloma, P;M., G. Trifirò, M.J. Schuemie, R. Gini, R. Herings, J. Hippisley-Cox et al. (2012), "Electronic Healthcare Databases for Active Drug Safety Surveillance: Is There Enough Leverage?", *Pharmacoepidemiology and Drug Safety*, Vol. 21, pp. 611-621.

El Emam, K. (2013), *Guide to the De-Identification of Personal Health Information*, Boca Raton.

European Collaboration for Healthcare Optimisation (2013), www.echo-health.eu/, accessed 14 September 2013.

Farr Institute (2014), www.farrinstitute.org/, accessed 12 August 2014.

FDA – US Food and Drug Administration (2013), "Mini-Sentinel", http://mini-sentinel.org/ accessed 13 September 2013.

Häkkinen, U., T. Iversen, M. Peltola, T.T. Seppälä, A. Malmivaara et al. (2013), "Health Care Performance Comparison Using a Disease-based Approach: The EuroHOPE Project", *Health Policy*, Vol. 112, No. 1–2, pp. 100-109.

Health Service Journal (2011), *HSJ Best Practice Awards 2011*, www.hsj.co.uk/journals/2011/11/21/o/c/i/HSJBP2011.pdf accessed 7 August 2014.

ICES – Institute for Clinical Evaluation Science (2013), "At a Glance: Evidence Guiding Health Care", www.ices.on.ca/webpage.cfm?site_id=1&org_id=70 accessed 13 September 2013.

Medical Research Council (2014), www.mrc.ac.uk/research/facilities/dementias-research-platform/, accessed 7 August 2014.

National Health Service (2014), www.nhs.uk/NHSEngland/thenhs/records/healthrecords/Pages/care-data.aspx, accessed 11 August 2014.

OECD (2015a), *Data Driven Innovation for Growth and Well-Being*, OECD, Paris, forthcoming.

OECD (2015b), "Governing Personal Health Data for Health Care Quality, Health System Performance and Research Innovation: Mechanisms and Tools for Privacy-Respectful Data Use" (working title), OECD Health Policy Studies, Paris, forthcoming.

OECD (2013a), *Strengthening Health Information Infrastructure for Health Care Quality Governance: Good Practices, New Opportunities and Data Privacy Protection Challenges*, OECD Health Policy Studies, OECD Publishing, Paris, http://dx.doi.org/10.1787/9789264193505-en.

OECD (2013b), *Addressing Dementia – The OECD Response*, www.oecd.org/sti/addressing-dementia-the-oecd-response.pdf.

SveDEM (2014), "Swedish Dementia Registry", www.ucr.uu.se/svedem/index.php/about-svedem accessed 12 August 2014.

Chapter 7

Benchmarking system performance in caring for dementia

Jeremy Veillard, Sara Guilcher, Abrar Salman and Geoff Anderson[1]

Governments face the daunting public policy challenge of dealing with the large and growing burden of dementia. High quality and sustainable systems of care for dementia will require innovation and profound changes in both financing mechanisms and health and social care delivery systems. To address this challenge, international performance comparisons and practice benchmarking systems are fundamental to support sound public policy development and shared learning from policy innovations. This chapter provides a conceptual framework for performance measurement of dementia care systems that can be used to map current international performance-comparison efforts, define gaps and guide efforts to fill those gaps. The chapter suggests that the World Health Organization (WHO) and the Organisation for Economic Co-operation and Development (OECD) engage their member countries in a co-ordinated and collaborative effort to share best practices for dementia care through practice benchmarking. The chaoter concludes that performance comparisons should be systematic and supported by relevant and valid information, interpreted in context and that practice benchmarking for dementia care systems will require substantial investments including the strengthening of health information systems.

7.1. Introduction

Dementia is a challenge to all governments in developed and low to middle income countries. The current burden of dementia is high and it is likely to increase over time as populations age (Hurd et al., 2013). In the face of this large and growing burden, there is a clear recognition that the existing health and social care delivery and financing models for dementia need to be improved. Providing appropriate, high quality, sustainable care for persons with dementia will require proper integration of health and social care services as well as appropriate support for informal caregivers. Governments will need to respond to the challenge by stimulating innovation, supporting and facilitating change management and sharing best practices.

In response to this emerging challenge, a number of international initiatives have taken place. In 2006, the Paris Declaration called on countries to make dementia a priority. The same year, Alzheimer Europe had adopted the declaration of the European Alzheimer movement. More recently, the G8 Summit on Dementia was held in the United Kingdom in December 2013 to set dementia as an international priority in order to find effective solutions to slow the impact of dementia on affected populations, their families and societies (Toosy, 2014). As a result of the G8 Summit, the World Dementia Council was created and held its first meeting in April 2014. The Council aims to stimulate innovation, development and commercialisation of life-enhancing drugs, treatments and care for people with dementia, or at risk of dementia (UK Department of Health, 2014). At the national level, several OECD countries have developed or are currently developing broad strategies to address the issue of dementia (for example the United Kingdom, France, Australia, New Zealand, the United States and Sweden). These strategies include innovative delivery models and financing mechanisms for formal and informal care.

Along with efforts to develop co-ordinated policy responses to dementia, early efforts to measure and benchmark on performance associated with dementia care have begun. These efforts include Alzheimer Europe's development of a set of quality indicators to monitor the performance of dementia care, including potential quality indicators, as well as indicators for formal and informal care providers (Alzheimer Europe, 2009); the RAND-led Assessing Care of Vulnerable Elders (ACOVE) (Wenger and Shekelle, 2001) project; the American Medical Association (AMA) development of a set of process quality indicators (Odenheimer et al., 2013); and the use of a number of indicators of quality of care and quality of life for dementia patients that can be derived from the InterRAI™ standards for mental health, home care and residential care in an increasing number of countries (Hirdes et al., 2008).

Building on these efforts will be important and there is a substantial opportunity for countries with sufficient health information infrastructure to work together to expand on current performance measurement efforts for dementia care systems. This effort will need to address important questions such as what types of indicators are needed in order to support international comparisons and benchmarking; what strategies can be mobilised to develop, implement and monitor performance for dementia care systems; and importantly what are the steps required for governments and international organisations to move forward in a proactive and collaborative manner.

In this context, there is an obvious role for governments to play in supporting the emergence of information systems for performance measurement and comparisons in dementia care systems. These systems will lead to a better understanding of how countries are performing in meeting the care and social needs of persons with dementia, as well as formal and informal caregivers. They will provide an opportunity for countries to compare the effectiveness of their policy initiatives analysed in their local contexts.

This chapter proposes a performance assessment framework for dementia care systems, and compares current performance measurement efforts to this framework; it also proposes concrete recommendations to set up performance and practice benchmarking mechanisms, as well as practical next steps for governments and international organisations to move forward in enhancing their benchmarking efforts for dementia care systems.

7.2. Assessing performance of dementia care systems

Conceptual performance assessment framework for dementia care systems

Goals for dementia care are broad and aim to maintain maximal cognitive and functional abilities, reduce the severity and frequency of behavioural and psychological symptoms, reduce the onset and impact of adverse events, minimise risks to health and safety, provide information and support to informal caregivers, and optimise the health and well-being of persons with dementia and informal caregivers (WHO, 2012). Globally, dementia care has been criticised for being reactive, unsystematic and fragmented (Odenheimer et al., 2013), and contributing to significant costs to the health and social care systems (Wimo and Prince, 2010). Several priorities for improvement and goal attainment have been identified including: raising awareness of dementia; timely diagnosis; commitment to quality care and service delivery; informal caregiver support; formal care training; prevention; and research (WHO, 2012).

A common conceptual performance measurement framework provides an opportunity to map out the different dimensions of performance that governments have to address concomitantly to effect change and improve performance for dementia care systems. Building on the conceptual frameworks of the OECD and the Institute for Healthcare Improvement (IHI), the Canadian Institute for Health Information (CIHI) developed and released in 2013 a conceptual framework for health system performance (CIHI, 2013). The framework covers fifteen dimensions of performance nested in four interrelated quadrants: 1) health system inputs and characteristics, 2) health system outputs, 3) social determinants of health, and 4) health system outcomes. In this paper we adapted CIHI's framework to dementia care systems. The adapted framework is presented in Figure 7.1 and its performance dimensions are described in more detail in Table 7.1.

Figure 7.1. Proposed system performance framework for dementia care systems

Political Context
Cultural Context
Social Determinants of Health
Structural factors influencing health
Biological, material, psychosocial and behavioural factors
Health System Inputs and Service Delivery
Leadership and governance for dementia care systems
Health system resources including financing mechanisms
Efficient allocation of resources
Adjustment to health needs of persons with dementia and caregivers
Health and social system innovation and learning capacity
Health System Outputs
Access to comprehensive and integrated health and social care services
Person-centred
Appropriate and effective
Safe
Efficiently delivered
Equity
Health System Outcomes
Improve health status including human function
Improve responsiveness of dementia care systems
Improve value for money
Equity
Demographic Context
Economic Context

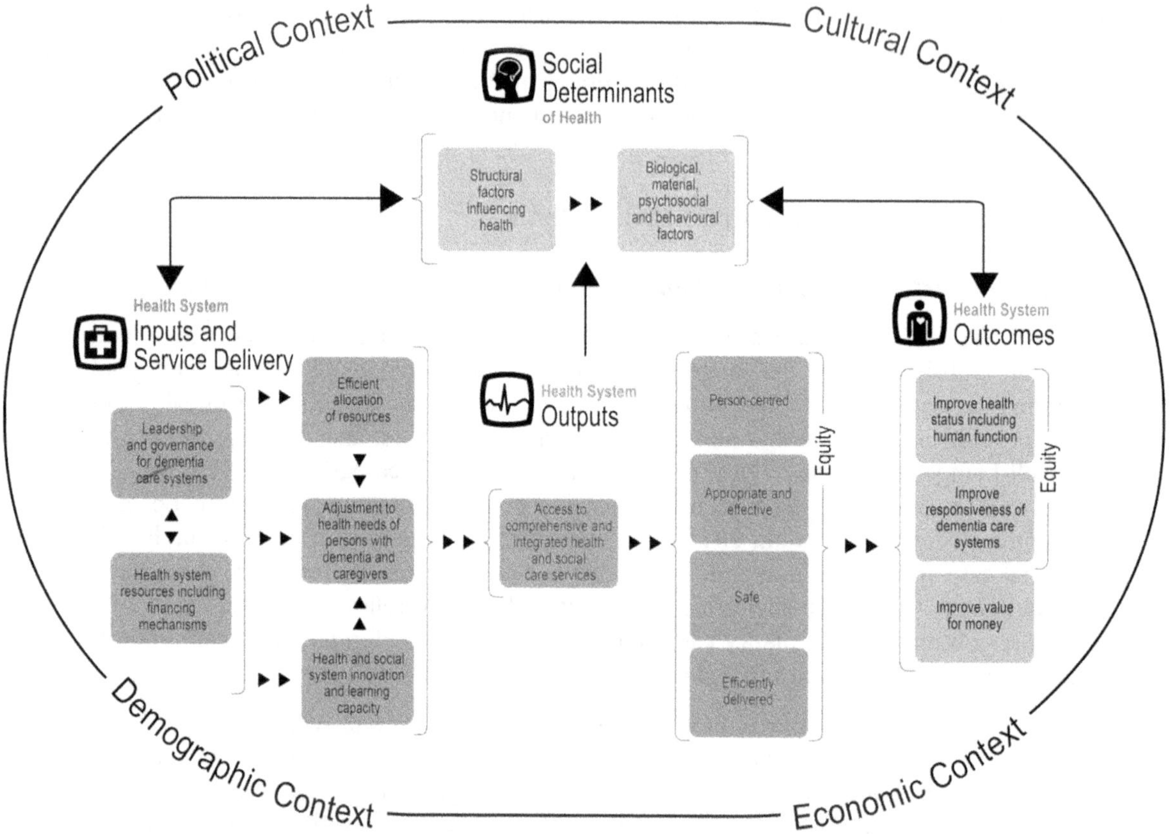

Table 7.1. Definitions of performance dimensions for dementia care systems

Performance quadrant	Performance dimension	Definition and examples
Health system inputs and characteristics	Leadership and governance for dementia care systems	Health system leadership and governance involve ensuring that strategic policy frameworks for dementia care systems exist and are combined with effective oversight, coalition-building, the provision of appropriate regulations and incentives, attention to system design, and accountability (Commission on Social Determinants of Health, 2008).
	Health system resources including financing mechanisms for dementia	Health system resources refer to the level of financial, human, physical (facilities), technical and informational (including the availability of high-quality data) resources available for dementia care systems.
	Efficient allocation of resources	Measures how resources are combined to produce health services to meet the population-based demands and needs of a society – in this case, persons with dementia and caregivers (Canadian Institute for Health Information 2012).
	Adjustment to health needs of persons with dementia and informal caregivers	Reflects the capacity of the health system to adapt to a changing environment of population health needs, in this case persons with dementia (Donabedian and Commonwealth Fund, 1973; Frenk and White, 1992; Long, 1994).
	Health and social system innovation in service delivery and learning capacity	Relates to the ability of dementia care systems to continuously improve services and implement new delivery models pertinent to the needs of patients with dementia and their caregivers (Damanpour and Evan, 1984).
Health system outputs	Access to comprehensive and integrated health and social care services	This dimension refers to the capacity of the health system to offer the range of health and social care services that meets the needs of persons with dementia and informal caregivers in a timely fashion without financial, organizational or geographical barriers to seeking or obtaining those services (Frenk and White, 1992).
	Person-centered care	Person-centered services are integrated services that support persons with dementia and their caregivers' experiences of continuity with health and social care services (Kodner, 2009; Shortell et al., 1993).
	Safe care	Safe health services are those that avoid injuring patients with the care that is intended to help them (US Institute of Medicine, 2001).
	Appropriate and effective care	Appropriateness and effectiveness of health services represent the main components of technical quality of care (Donabedian, 1980) and are based on the application of current scientific knowledge and clinical norms to achieve the most favorable balance of risks and benefits for dementia patients.
	Efficiently delivered care	Efficiently delivered health and social care services correspond to the technical efficiency of the health system and refer to maximising outputs (services) for a given level and mix of inputs (resources), or minimising the inputs used to deliver a given level and mix of outputs.
Health system outcomes	Improve health status of patients with dementia and their caregivers	Health status of individuals and the population covers three components: health conditions, health function, and well-being.
	Improve responsiveness of dementia care system	The health system must provide services and improve population health in a way that meets the needs and expectations of the people it serves in accordance with societal values (Murray and Frenk, 2000).
	Improve value for money	Value for money is related to the outcomes, responsiveness and equity of dementia care systems. It is a measure of the level of achievement of these three goals compared with the resources used (Murray and Frenk, 2000).
Social determinants of health	Structural determinants	Structural factors influencing health are those that shape the socioeconomic position of persons with dementia and their families, socioeconomic position, such as income and social status, education and literacy, and gender and ethnicity.
	Intermediary determinants	Biological factors include genes, aging processes and sex-linked biology. Material circumstances include characteristics of neighbourhoods, housing, working conditions and the physical environment (WHO, 2008, 2010; Government of Canada, 1994, 1999). Psychosocial circumstances include stress, an individual's sense of control and social support networks (Wilkinson and Marmot; 2003; Government of Canada, 1999; Cassel, 1976). Behavioural factors include such things as smoking, physical exercise, diet and nutrition (WHO, 2008, 2010; Wilkinson and Marmot; 2003; Government of Canada, 1999; Cassel, 1976; Lynch et al., 2001), and all factors that may influence dementia (Barnes and Yaffe, 2011)

7.3. Using the system performance framework for dementia care systems to map current indicators

Several countries including the United States, the United Kingdom, and Australia, have started developing quality indicators and minimum standards for dementia care systems. In the United States, the Dementia Measures Work Group (DWG) recommended ten process measures at the clinical level to improve outcomes for persons with dementia (American Medical Association, 2011, 2014; Odenheimer et al., 2013). The United Kingdom's National Institute for Health and Care Excellence (NICE) has developed quality standards for any health and social formal care provider who is in direct contact with persons with dementia. Recently, three new additional indicators have been recommended, which relate to frequent memory assessments and blood testing for persons with dementia, and the identification of informal care provider(s) on a medical record. The NICE menu of indicators is similar to the set proposed by Alzheimer Europe, an organisation which represents 36 Alzheimer associations from 31 countries across Europe.

Still, there are many challenges related to performance measurement of dementia care systems. Many of the performance measurement activities for dementia have focused on measuring *health system outputs* (e.g., *clinical quality and appropriateness*) rather than other domains of performance measurement (Smith, 2009), such as system inputs, health system outcomes and social determinants of health (American Medical Association, 2011; Odenheimer et al., 2013, Alzheimer Europe, 2009). From that perspective, using a conceptual framework to map indicators to performance domains is a helpful step to define a more robust core set of key performance indicators for benchmarking dementia care systems.

There has also been difficulty defining clinical outcomes due to the limited evidence of the impact of existing interventions on disease progression (American Medical Association, 2011; WHO, 2012; Rabins et al., 2007). Despite the lack of evidence in delaying clinical outcomes for the progression of dementia, there are opportunities for health systems to focus on improving other domains of performance measurement (Smith, 2009). This is particularly true of system outcomes such as *responsiveness of the health system* and *self-reported health status* with patient and family experience and satisfaction measures (Smith, 2009; Herrmann and Gauthier, 2008). In particular, patient reported outcome measures (PROMs) may fill the current gap in dementia-related outcomes and assist with informed decision making based on patient experience (Marshall et al., 2006).

Finally, the importance of patient and family engagement is well documented in dementia process indicators (e.g., Alzheimer's Europe, 2009); however, there remains a notable absence of indicators addressing such engagement-related outcomes. The DWG in the United States proposed several outcomes related to the concept of engagement for future consideration, such as promoting caregiver and patient-centered decision making, reducing caregiver stress and burden, improving quality of life, and enhancing caregiver involvement and comfort with dementia care (American Medical Association, 2011).

An important potential use of the performance framework for dementia care systems is that it provides a way to map out current international performance measurement efforts, as a way to define commonalities and information gaps. Table 7.2 is a first attempt at mapping out international performance measurement efforts for dementia care systems and identifying possible new indicators to fill in existing performance measurement gaps. New indicators proposed are indicated in italic.

Table 7.2. Potential performance indicators for dementia care systems

Performance dimension	Examples of initiatives related to this dimension	Performance indicators *(proposed new indicators in italic)*
Leadership and governance for dementia care systems	National dementia care strategies	*Number of countries with dementia strategy* *Number of countries with dementia friends programme*
Health system resources including financing mechanisms for dementia	Tax benefits program for caregivers	*Percentage of patients and caregivers population precipitated in catastrophic health and social care expenditures* *Percentage of caregivers leaving the workforce to care for person with dementia* *Percentage of dementia friendly homes available to persons diagnosed with dementia who are eligible for housing modifications*
Efficient allocation of resources	Dementia care training for formal care providers	*Percentage of primary care providers trained in early diagnosis and ongoing treatment of dementia* *Inclusion of dementia related curriculum in health professional training* Percentage of staff at a care service/facility that receive specific dementia-care training on a regular basis, at least once a year (American Medical Association) *Percentage of clinicians, services/facilities, that adopt diagnosis guidelines* *Licensure standards permit delegation of duties as appropriate*
Adjustment to health needs of persons with dementia and informal caregivers	Monitoring of disease progression	Percentage of patients, regardless of age, with a diagnosis of dementia whose caregiver(s) were provided with education on dementia disease management and health behavior changes and referred to additional resources for support within a 12 month period (American Medical Association)
Health and social system innovation in service delivery and learning capacity for dementia	Dementia-friendly housing	*Percentage of cognitively impaired in clinical trials* *Assistive technologies with proven benefits and cost-effectiveness come to market*
Access to comprehensive and integrated health and social care services		*Percentage of estimated population with, or at risk for, dementia that are receiving cognitive assessment or formal diagnosis* *Access to validated and standardized cognitive assessment and diagnostic tools* *Time between onset of clinical symptoms, clinical detection and diagnosis*
Person-centered care	Person-centered care plans	Percentage of persons with a diagnosis of dementia who have a registration of an updated care plan including life history, social and family circumstances, preferences (diet, sexuality, religion) (Alzheimer Europe) and involving families and caregivers Percentage of persons with dementia whose care plan includes both activities of daily living and recreational, social, leisure and structured day activities (Alzheimer Europe) *Progressive improvement in the well-being of those receiving quality care services over those who do not*
Safe care	Counselling regarding risks of driving	*Rates of adverse events for people with dementia (pressure ulcers, falls)* Percentage of patients, regardless of age, with a diagnosis of dementia or their caregiver(s) who were counselled regarding the risks of driving and the alternatives to driving at least once within a 12 month period (American Medical Association)
Appropriate and effective care	Neuropsychiatric symptom assessment	*Percentage of population diagnosed with dementia living at home at different stages of disease evolution* *Percentage of long term care residents prescribed antipsychotic drugs without a diagnosis of* *Percentage of patients with dementia dying at home* *Percentage reporting satisfaction with their at-home care in surveys*
Efficiently delivered care	Staging of dementia	*Percentage of regions that have achieved cost-effectiveness in dementia care (e.g., improved diagnosis and community services, reductions of unnecessary transitions into care homes and shorter length of stays in acute care)*
Health status	Patient and family experience	Perceived quality of life and well-being for people with dementia Percentage of caregivers with poor quality of life and inability to cope *Percentage of patients and/or family who are satisfied with their formal health care experiences*
System responsiveness	Accreditation	*Percentage of services/facilities that have achieved minimum standards for dementia patients (e.g., accreditation)*
Value for money	Spend to save	*Percentage of regions that have achieved cost-effectiveness in dementia care (e.g., improved diagnosis and community services, reductions of unnecessary transitions into care homes and shorter length of stays in acute care)*
Structural determinants	Health in all policies	*Percentage of regions with a health in all policy approach for dementia care*
Intermediary determinants	Screening for risk factors	*Percentage of total health expenditures invested in health promotion activities targeting cardio-vascular diseases* *Percentage of patients in primary health care who are screened annually for risk factors related to dementia (e.g., hypertension, obesity, alcohol, smoking, stroke)*

Building on this extensive list of performance indicators, it seemed helpful to provide an example of what could constitute a core set of a dozen performance indicators for benchmarking dementia care systems. Table 7.3 below presents the core set of 12 key performance indicators balanced across the various performance dimensions of the framework and mapped to key policy questions related to the performance of dementia care systems.

Table 7.3. Example of a potential core set of performance indicators for benchmarking dementia care systems

Key policy question	Examples of key performance indicators
Do people with dementia receive person-centered, appropriate and safe care?	1. Percentage of population diagnosed with dementia living at home at different stages of disease evolution 2. Percentage of long term care residents prescribed antipsychotic drugs without a diagnosis of psychosis 3. Percentage of patients with dementia dying at home 4. Perceived quality of life and well-being for people with dementia
Does every person diagnosed with dementia receive an individualized care plan updated regularly and involving families and caregivers?	5. Percentage of estimated population with, or at risk for, dementia that are receiving cognitive assessment or formal diagnosis 6. Percentage of persons with a diagnosis of dementia who have a registration of an updated care plan including life history, social and family circumstances, preferences (diet, sexuality, religion) (Alzheimer Europe) and involving families and caregivers
Are caregivers provided with support services allowing them to cope with the care they have to deliver to people with dementia?	7. Percentage of caregivers with poor quality of life and inability to cope
Are people with dementia and caregivers becoming impoverished because they have dementia or have to care for people with dementia?	8. Percentage of patients and caregivers affected by catastrophic health and social care expenditures 9. Percentage of caregivers leaving the workforce to care for person with dementia
Are sufficient resources in promoting appropriate health behaviours protective of dementia?	10. Percentage of total health expenditures invested in health promotion activities targeting cardio-vascular diseases
Are front line workers appropriately trained to deliver high quality care to people with dementia?	11. Percentage of primary care providers trained in early diagnosis and ongoing treatment of dementia
Do research and care delivery innovation involve cognitively impaired population?	12. Percentage of cognitively impaired in clinical trials

Performance measurement of dementia care systems is in its early days; however there is an important role for countries and international organisations such as the OECD and the WHO to play in defining a framework for performance measurement and selecting key performance indicators that can be used for international comparisons and benchmarking. Collecting the data supporting these performance indicators will require investments in information systems and the development of new methods, particularly for patient reported outcomes. Still, there are short term opportunities to fill information gaps through the use of national survey instruments, administrative data, as well as clinical data when minimum content standards and data sets have been defined and implemented and information is collected and available.

7.4. Investing in practice benchmarking to accelerate the emergence and spread of effective policy interventions at national level in OECD countries

Complementing performance benchmarking with practice benchmarking for dementia care systems

At the G8 dementia summit hosted in London in December 2013, G8 member states agreed to work together to build an international effort to double funding for dementia research, to increase the number of people involved in clinical trials and to work towards a cure or disease-modifying therapy for dementia by 2025. Along with a commitment to cure research, the G8 tasked the WHO and the OECD with supporting countries to strengthen health and social care systems to improve care and services for people with dementia (Toosy, 2014). The development of performance comparisons and benchmarking is crucial for dementia care systems where the stakes are high and appropriate and effective public policies are still largely undefined.

In particular, a well-designed benchmarking system has the potential to guide policy development and can be used both prospectively and retrospectively (Veillard, 2012). It can support better understanding of past performance and the rationale behind certain performance patterns (retrospective use) and also help to revise strategies for improving future performance (prospective use). Despite challenges to international benchmarking related to data issues, there are lessons learned that can be applied to health systems and seem particularly pertinent to the development of international benchmarking systems for dementia care. A key to the success of performance comparisons and practice benchmarking is the need to factor in context and challenges related to change management.

More practically, it has been suggested that benchmarking of health systems should meet the following requirements: focus on practice as well as performance; use beyond evaluating and comparing performance; reflect a broader change process; focus on strategic priorities, involve clear and careful planning, and best practices, and adapt to local context; and finally provide links between resource allocation and benchmark performance (Neely, 2013). The policy-focus of this vision of international benchmarking is consistent with a minimum set of characteristics defined for strategy-based health system performance benchmarking systems, outlined in Table 7.4 (Veillard, 2012).

Table 7.4. Key characteristics of strategy-based health system performance benchmarking systems

Key characteristic	Definition
Strategic focus	The link between health system strategies and international benchmarking efforts ensures that policy lessons will be designed for those who can act upon the findings.
Adaptability and flexibility	Benchmarking efforts can undertake both large (full health systems comparisons) and narrower scope studies, using tools that can be administered in a time frame that matches the agenda of policy makers.
Data standardization	Efforts are made to standardize data and facilitate credible comparisons.
Policy focus rather than research focus	Benchmarking systems are not driven by experts or researchers but by policy-makers supported by experts and researchers.
Efforts to translate performance information and policy lessons for decision makers	Innovative analytical tools are used to represent performance information in rigorous yet explicit ways, conveying data in a meaningful manner.
Sensitivity to political and contextual issues	Interpretation of indicator data should not lose sight of the policy context within which performance is measured; of the players involved in formulating and implementing policy; of the time lag needed to assess the impact of different policies; and of aspects of health care that remain unmeasured by available data.

Moving forward on performance and practice benchmarking for dementia care systems

There are a number of practical steps that can help countries move forward in sharing best practices in ways that are focused on key aspects of dementia care systems performance and can accelerate the spread of innovation at national levels.

A key first step to be considered would be for the OECD and the WHO to engage their member states in a collaborative and co-ordinated discussion of performance measurement for dementia care systems that identifies a common conceptual framework which could be used to highlight gaps in existing information systems and to develop strategies to address current gaps. A second step would be to initiate and structure practice benchmarking efforts on key strategic aspects of dementia care systems. The focus could be on key policy issues that are currently dilemmas for governments, such as: the timely diagnosis of dementia care (which raises significant practical and ethical challenges); the financing of dementia care, which is still inadequate and for which an integrated approach is needed to face up to the growing financial burden of dementia; the profound changes required in health and social care delivery models; and finally the need for minimum standards for quality of dementia care systems.

This work needs to be started rapidly, perhaps with a small group of countries (e.g., France, the United Kingdom, Australia and Canada) that are more advanced in defining their range of policy interventions leading the way and then expanded, as momentum builds over time. It will be important to complement information on policy innovations and performance improvement with a documentation of contextual elements related to the implementation of innovative policy interventions, change management and evaluation frameworks and results. Finally, it will be critical to ensure that scientific rigour is built into practice benchmarking and that resources can be gathered and shared efficiently.

As part of this effort, national governments will need to invest in information systems and international comparability of data as well as in the practice benchmarking efforts proposed above. International organisations will need to ensure the validity of international performance information, and the scientific rigour of practice benchmarking efforts. Both national governments and international organisations will need to work closely with civil society, the industry and in particular patients and caregivers' associations to maximise the scale and spread of benchmarking efforts.

Understanding the full scope of government interventions in dementia care systems

It is important for countries interested in performance and practice benchmarking to understand the scope of their stewardship function in dementia care. Well-functioning dementia care systems require the co-ordination and integration of health and social care services and policies to support informal caregivers. Table 7.5 below can serve as a guide for national health ministries to review the effectiveness of their health system stewardship function in better meeting the health and social services needs of dementia patients and of their caregivers.

Table 7.5. Application of generic health system stewardship functions of health ministries to dementia care systems

Generic health system stewardship functions of health ministries	Application to dementia care systems
To define the strategy for achieving better population health	Defining a vision for health for people with dementia and their caregivers, drawing up a strategy and co-ordinated policies, and defining and mobilising the resources required to attain desired goals
To exert influence across all sectors through intersectoral collaboration and action in order to promote better health for dementia patients	National health ministries can play various roles to influence secondary and tertiary factors affecting dementia care systems and dementia risk factors, such as: building coalitions across sectors in government, and with actors outside government, to achieve better dementia care systems; promoting initiatives aimed at improving health for dementia patients or addressing related social determinants of health; and advocating for the incorporation of health issues in all policies.
To enhance governance and accountability	Consists in ensuring that national health ministries govern the health sector in a way that is fair, ethical, and conducive to the attainment of health system goals. Governance is reflected in the relationship between the state and citizens, in the structural reporting relationships in the health system, and in the contractual and other instruments that health system actors can use to ensure goal attainment and the broader alignment of the behaviours of system stakeholders with the goal of improving dementia care systems.
To ensure alignment of health system design with health system goals	Requires that health ministries ensure a fit between strategy and institutional and organisational structure, and that there are efforts in place to reduce system duplication and fragmentation. It also implies that the health system has the capacity to adapt its strategies and policies to take into account changing priorities and health needs.
To ensure the effective and appropriate use of legal, regulatory, and policy instruments to implement health system strengthening strategies	The achievement of an effective and comprehensive mix and allocation of powers, incentives, guidelines, best practices, and sanctions with which to steer the performance of government's agents and of the actors in the broader health sector.
To ensure the collection, dissemination, and application of appropriate health information and research evidence	This includes the combined use of epidemiological, economic, performance data and research evidence.

Source: Veillard, J. (2012), "Performance Management in Health Systems and Services", Studies on its Development and Use at International, National/Jurisdictional, and Hospital Levels.

7.5. Conclusion

The emergence of dementia as a priority issue for public policy requires not only investments in research to find a cure, but also a commitment to improvement in financing mechanisms and health and social care delivery systems for people with dementia and their caregivers. Meeting this commitment requires systematic thinking about performance measurement and practice benchmarking for the functions of health ministries and the broader government functions crucial to successful dementia care systems. It will also require investing in information systems and methods development to collect information that is standardised and comparable across countries.

From this perspective, international comparisons play an important role because they have the potential to accelerate the understanding and implementation of innovative solutions. However, these comparisons need to be supported by relevant and valid information, and interpreted in context. Performance benchmarking efforts will benefit from the experience of the OECD and the WHO in this area. Practice benchmarking is more challenging but has the potential to stimulate and accelerate the spread and scale up of innovations in service delivery, financing and coverage. Dementia care systems offer a unique opportunity for countries with similar emerging problems to learn from one another. This will require substantial investments – particularly in strengthening health information systems – but the stakes are so high that such investments seem both timely and opportune.

Note

1. This chapter has been written by Jeremy Veillard, PhD, Canadian Institute for Health Information, Toronto, Canada and Institute for Health Policy, Management and Evaluation, University of Toronto, Canada; Sara Guilcher, PT, PhD, Canadian Institute for Health Information, Toronto and Li Ka Shing Knowledge Institute, St. Michael's Hospital, Toronto, Canada; Abrar Salman, MHI, Canadian Institute for Health Information, Toronto, Canada; Geoff Anderson, MD, PhD, Institute for Health Policy, Management and Evaluation, University of Toronto, Canada.

   Corresponding author: Jeremy Veillard, PhD, Vice-President, Research and Analysis, Canadian Institute for Health Information, Toronto.

References

Alzheimer Europe (2009), "Potential Quality Indicators".

American Medical Association (2014), "Dementia Performance Measurement Set".

American Medical Association (2011), "Dementia Performance Measurement Set".

Barnes, D.E. and K. Yaffe (2011), "The Projected Effect of Risk Factor Reduction on Alzheimer's Disease Prevalence", *The Lancet Neurology*, Vol. 10, No. 9.

Cassel, J. (1976), "The Contribution of the Social Environment to Host Resistance", *American Journal of Epidemiology*, Vol. 104, No. 2.

CIHI – Canadian Institute for Health Information (2013), "A Performance Measurement Framework for the Canadian Health System".

Commission on Social Determinants of Health (2008), "Closing the Gap in a Generation: Health Equity Through Action on the Social Determinants of Health: Final Report of the Commission on Social Determinants of Health", World Health Organization, Geneva.

Damanpour, F. and W.M. Evan (1984), "Organizational Innovation and Performance: The Problem of 'Organizational lag'", *Administrative Science Quarterly*.

Donabedian, A. (1980), "The Definition of Quality and Approaches to its Assessment", Health Administration, Michigan Press, An Arbor 1.

Donabedian, A. and the Commonwealth Fund (1973), *Aspects of Medical Care Administration: Specifying Requirements for Health Care*, Harvard University Press, Cambridge.

Frenk, J. and K.L. White (1992), "The Concept and Measurement of Accessibility", PAHO Scientific Publication, Pan-American Health Organization.

Government of Canada (1994), "Strategies for Population Health. Investing in the Health of Canadians".

Government of Canada. Territorial Advisory Committee on Population Health (1999), "Toward a Healthy Future: Second Report on the Health of Canadians", Vol. 117.

Herrmann, N. and S. Gauthier (2008), "Diagnosis and Treatment of Dementia: 6. Management of Severe Alzheimer Disease", *Canadian Medical Association Journal*, Vol. 179, No. 12.

Hirdes, J.P. et al. (2008), "Reliability of the InterRAI Suite of Assessment Instruments: A 12-country Study of an Integrated Health Information System", *BMC Health Services Research*, Vol. 8.

Hurd, M.D. et al. (2013), "Monetary Costs of Dementia in the United States", *New England Journal of Medicine*, Vol. 368, No. 14.

Kodner, D.L. (2009), "All Together Now: A Conceptual Exploration of Integrated Care", *Healthcare Quarterly,* Vol. 13.

Long, M.J. (1994), *The Medical Care System: A Conceptual Model*, AUPHA Press, Health Administration Press.

Lynch, J. et al. (2001), "Income Inequality, the Psychosocial Environment, and Health: Comparisons of Wealthy Nations", *The Lancet*, Vol. 358, No. 9277.

Marshall, S., K. Haywood and R. Fitzpatrick (2006), "Impact of Patient-reported Outcome Measures on Routine Practice: A Structured Review", *Journal of Evaluation in Clinical Practice*, Vol. 12, No. 5.

Murray, C. and J. Frenk (2000), "A Framework for Assessing the Performance of Health Systems", *Bulletin of the World Health Organization*, Vol. 78, No. 6.

Neely, A. (2013), "Benchmarking: Lessons and Implications for Health Systems1", *Health System Performance Comparison: An Agenda For Policy, Information and Research.*

Odenheimer, G. et al. (2013), "Quality Improvement in Neurology Dementia Management Quality Measures", *Neurology*, Vol. 81, No. 17.

Rabins, P.V., D. Blacker and B.W. Rovner (2007), "APA Work Group on Alzheimer Disease and other Dementias. Steering Committee on Practice Guidelines, American Psychiatric Association practice guideline for the treatment of patients with Alzheimer disease and other dementias", *American Journal of Psychiatry*, Vol. 164, No. 12.

Shortell, S.M. et al. (1993), "Creating Organized Delivery Systems: The Varriers and Facilitators", Hospital and Health Services Administration.

Smith, P.C. (2009), *Performance Measurement for Health System Improvement: Experiences, Challenges and Prospects*, Cambridge University Press.

Toosy, A.T. (2014), "G8 Dementia Summit: A Chance for United Action", *Journal Cover 13.1.*

UK Department of Health (2014), "World Dementia Council Meets for the First Time".

US Institute of Medicine (2001), *Crossing the Quality Chasm: A New Health System for the 21st Century*, National Academies Press.

Veillard, J. (2012), "Performance Management in Health Systems and Services", Studies on its Development and Use at International, National/Jurisdictional, and Hospital Levels.

Wenger, N.S. and P.G. Shekelle (2001), "Assessing Care of Vulnerable Elders: ACOVE Project Overview", *Annals of Internal Medicine*, Vol. 135, No. 8, Part 2.

Wilkinson, R.G. and M.G. Marmot (2003), "Social Determinants of Health: the Solid Facts", World Health Organization.

Wimo, A. and M.J. Prince (2010), "World Alzheimer Report 2010: The Global Economic Impact of Dementia", Alzheimer's Disease International.

WHO – World Health Organization (2012), *Dementia: A Public Health Priority,* WHO, Geneva.

WHO (2010), "A Conceptual Framework for Action on Social Determinants of Health", Social Determinants of Health Discussion Paper No. 2 (Policy and Practice), WHO, Geneva.

WHO (2008), "Closing the Gap in a Generation: Health Equity Through Action on the Social Determinants of Health", WHO, Geneva.

Annex A. Workshop agenda

Addressing dementia research and care: Can big data help?

Sunday September 14th 2014
The Faculty Club
Main Lounge
41 Willcocks Street, Toronto, Ontario

5:30–9:00pm	**Open Reception** Doors open at 5:30, Remarks at 6:00

Monday September 15th 2014
The Carlu
Round Room
444 Yonge Street, Toronto, Ontario
7th Floor

8:00–8:30am	*Continental Breakfast*
	Opening Remarks
8:30–8:35am	Minister Reza Moridi, Ministry of Research and Innovation
8:35–8:45am	Dirk Pilat, OECD
8:45-8:50am	**Context and Perspectives** Moderator: Donald Stuss, Ontario Brain Institute
8:50-9:00am	**Perspectives from the Global CEO Initiative** George Vradenburg, Global CEO Initiative
9:00-9:10am	**Updates from the World Dementia Council and G7 Legacy Workshop** Yves Joanette, CIHR
9:10-9:20am	**Perspectives from the OECD** Francesca Colombo, OECD
9:20-9:25am	**What are the new opportunities from big data to improve treatment and care?** Moderator: Geoff Anderson
9:25-9:40am	**Opportunities for Government** Adalsteinn Brown, IHPME
9:40-9:55am	**Opportunities for Researchers** Peter St. George-Hyslop, University of Toronto
9:55-10:10am	**Opportunities for Business, Foundations and Stakeholders** John Alam, EIP Pharma

10:10-10:25am	**Group Discussion and Lessons Learned**
10:25-10:45am	*Morning Break*
10:45-10:50am	**Are data available and useable? What are the key challenges and opportunities?** Moderator: Creighton Phelps, National Institute on Aging
10:50-11:20am	**Big Data for Dementia - OECD Perspectives** Robin Buckle, MRC and Eric Meyer, Oxford Internet Institute
11:20-11:50am	**The OBI Example - Brain-CODE and Data Federation** Donald Stuss, OBI
11:50-12:10pm	**Lessons learned from US-ADNI and GAAIN** Maria Carrillo, Alzheimer's Association
12:10-12:30pm	**Group Discussion and Lessons Learned**
12:30-1:30pm	*Lunch*
1:30-1:35pm	**Establishing systems to use big data for health policy and care.** Moderator: Michael Schull, ICES
1:35-1:50pm	**Privacy by Design: An International Framework** Ann Cavoukian, Institute for Privacy and Big Data
1:50-2:05pm	**OECD Data Privacy and Access** Jillian Oderkirk, OECD
2:05-2:35pm	**Benchmarking System Performance in Caring for Dementia** Jeremy Veillard, CIHI
2:35-3:00pm	Group Discussion and Lessons Learned
3:00-3:30pm	*Afternoon Break*
	Data-driven health innovation: Next steps for Canada, the OECD, and the world. Moderator: Dirk Pilat, OECD
3:30-4:30pm	**Moderated Panel Discussion of Next Steps to Advance Data-driven Innovation** Deputy Minister Bob Bell, Ministry of Health and Long-term Care Elettra Ronchi, OECD Francesca Colombo, OECD Robyn Tamblyn, CIHR Rick Johnson, BIAC George Vradenburg, Global CEO Initiative
4:30-5:00pm	**Attendees Questions to Panel and General Discussion**
5:00-5:15pm	**Closing Summary and Comments** OECD
5:15-5:30pm	**Closing Remarks and Highlights** Honorary Chair: Mr. Joseph Rotman

Please feel free to join us after the workshop at 6:30 for the public talk:

"The Activist's Imperative:
How to Drive Urgency and Unity in the Work of Halting Alzheimer's"
with George Vradenburg

Tuesday September 16th 2014

MaRS Discovery District
Collaboration Room 3
101 College Street, Toronto, Ontario

8:00–9:00am	Continental Breakfast and Tour of MaRS Discovery District
9:00–10:00am	Optum Labs Demonstration
10:00-1:00pm	Post-workshop Working Group

Sponsored by:

Alzheimer Society
CANADA

Annex B
Participants in the workshop

Name	Organisation	Country
Allison Barr	Ministry of Research and Innovation	Canada (Ontario)
Ann Cavoukian	Institute of Big Data and Privacy, Ryerson University	Canada
Anne Fazzalari	Canada Health Infoway	Canada
Barry Greenberg	University Health Network	Canada
Bill Mantel	Ministry of Research and Innovation	Canada (Ontario)
Bob Bell	Ministry of Health and Long Term Care	Canada (Ontario)
Bradley Buchsbaum	Rotman Research Institute	Canada
David O'Toole	Canadian Institute for Health Information	Canada
Denise Taylor-Gilhen	Parkinson Society Eastern Ontario	Canada
Dirk Pilat	OECD	France
Don Stuss	Ontario Brain Institute	Canada
Drew Holzapfel	High Lantern Group	United States
Elettra Ronchi	OECD	France
Eric Meyer	Oxford Internet Institute	United Kingdom
Francesca Colombo	OECD	France
Gale Carey	Alzheimer Society of Ontario	Canada
Geoff Anderson	Institute of Health Policy, Management and Evaluation, University of Toronto	Canada
George Vradenburg	Global CEO Initiative on Alzheimer's Disease	United Kingdom
Herve Lilliu	UCB	Belgium
Howard Hu	Dalla Lana School of Public Health, University of Toronto	Canada
Isabella Beretta	State Secretariat for Education, Research and Innovation	Switzerland
James Beck	Home Instead Senior Care	United States
Jane Aubin	Canadian Institutes of Health Research	Canada
Jeremy Veillard	Canadian Institute for Health Information	Canada
Jillian Oderkirk	OECD	France
John Alam	EIP Pharma	United States
John Lemberger	Ministry of Health	Israel
Joseph Rotman	Ontario Brain Institute	Canada
Karen Michell	Council of Academic Hospitals	Canada
Ken Evans	Ontario Brain Institute	Canada
Ken Rockwood	Dalhousie University	Canada
Kirk Nylen	Ontario Brain Institute	Canada
Steve Marcella	Merck	United States
Maria Carrillo	Alzheimer's Association	United States
Martin Rossor	University College London	United Kingdom
Matthew Norton	IMS Brogan	Canada
Michael Schull	Institute for Clinical and Evaluative Sciences	Canada
Michael Strong	Western University	Canada
Mike Simmons	Eli Lilly	United States
Mimi Lowi-Young	Alzheimer Society Canada	Canada
Nancy Kennedy	Ministry of Health and Long Term Care	Canada (Ontario)
Creighton Phelps	National Institute on Aging	United States
Neil Seeman	Dalla Lana School of Public Health, University of Toronto	Canada
Parminder Raina	Canadian Longitudinal Study on Aging	Canada
Paul Wallace	Optum Labs	United States
Paulo Jorge Nogueira	Directorate of Analysis and Information	Portugal
Peter St George-Hyslop	Tanz Neuroscience, University of Toronto	Canada
Minister Reza Moridi	Ministry of Research and Innovation	Canada (Ontario)
Robin Buckle	Medical Research Council	United Kingdom
Robyn Tamblyn	Canadian Institutes of Health Research	Camada
Ronni Gamzu	Ministry of Health	Israel
Roza Hayduk	Quintiles	United States
Saira Meese-Tamuri	Sunnybrook Hospital	Canada
Sandra Black	Sunnybrook Hospital	Canada
Scott Wallace	Optum Labs	United States
Sean Hill	International Neuroinformatics Coordinating Facility	Sweden
Shiva Amiri	Ontario Brain Institute	Canada
Steini Brown	Institute of Health Policy, Management and Evaluation	Canada
Steven Johnson	OneMind for Research	United States
Ulrike Rauer	Oxford Internet Institute	United Kingdom
Vaibhav Narayan	Johnson & Johnson	United States
Vanessa Foran	Parkinsons Society Canada	Canada
Yoshiaki Tojo	Japan External Trade Organisation	Japan
Yves Joanette	Canadian Institutes of Health Research	Canada
Zaven Katchatrurian	Alzheimer's Association	United States

ORGANISATION FOR ECONOMIC CO-OPERATION AND DEVELOPMENT

The OECD is a unique forum where governments work together to address the economic, social and environmental challenges of globalisation. The OECD is also at the forefront of efforts to understand and to help governments respond to new developments and concerns, such as corporate governance, the information economy and the challenges of an ageing population. The Organisation provides a setting where governments can compare policy experiences, seek answers to common problems, identify good practice and work to co-ordinate domestic and international policies.

The OECD member countries are: Australia, Austria, Belgium, Canada, Chile, the Czech Republic, Denmark, Estonia, Finland, France, Germany, Greece, Hungary, Iceland, Ireland, Israel, Italy, Japan, Korea, Luxembourg, Mexico, the Netherlands, New Zealand, Norway, Poland, Portugal, the Slovak Republic, Slovenia, Spain, Sweden, Switzerland, Turkey, the United Kingdom and the United States. The European Union takes part in the work of the OECD.

OECD Publishing disseminates widely the results of the Organisation's statistics gathering and research on economic, social and environmental issues, as well as the conventions, guidelines and standards agreed by its members.

OECD PUBLISHING, 2, rue André-Pascal, 75775 PARIS CEDEX 16
(81 2015 02 1 P) ISBN 978-92-64-22841-2 – 2015

www.ingramcontent.com/pod-product-compliance
Lightning Source LLC
LaVergne TN
LVHW081412110826
845149LV00010B/1712

* 9 7 8 9 2 6 4 2 2 8 4 1 2 *